DRUM COLORS

by Rob Cook

Second Edition

© 2022 by Rob Cook

ISBN   978-1-888408-57-7

Rebeats
P.O. Box 6, Alma, Michigan 48801
www.Rebeats.com

Printed in the United States of America
All rights for publication and distribution are reserved. No part of this book may be reproduced in any form or by any electronic of mechanical means including information storage and retrieval systems without publisher's written consent.

Camco	1
Fibes	6
Gretsch	7
Leedy	19
Ludwig	29
Rogers	51
Slingerland	57

CAMCO

Colors were not listed in catalogs until 1964. In the earlier catalogs, there was simply annotation next to drums and outfits that they were available in a choice of lacquer or pearl finishes, or, in the case of some snare and parade drums, in mahogany finish.

The 1963 catalog featured drums with all the available finishes on the front cover, but the colors were still not listed in the catalog. "Moire" finishes were $30 extra. (Moire finishes included what is commonly referred to today as "Satin Flame" finishes.

CAMCO

RED SPARKLE	BLUE SPARKLE	CHAMPAGNE SPARKLE	SILVER SPARKLE	BURGUNDY SPARKLE
BLUE RIPPLE	GRAY RIPPLE	GREEN SPARKLE	GOLD SPARKLE	OYSTER
BLACK DIAMOND	WHITE PEARL	BLUE MOIRE	CHARCOAL MOIRE	AQUA MOIRE
CHROME MOIRE	GOLD MOIRE	PURPLE MOIRE	RED MOIRE	3-D MOIRE

EBONY STAIN	CLEAR MAPLE	MOSS GREEN STAIN	WALNUT STAIN

1964 Catalog color swatches
select snare and parade drums were also still offered in lacquered finishes

EBONY STAIN	CLEAR MAPLE	WALNUT STAIN	MOSS GREEN STAIN	RED STAIN

1967 Colors were essentially the same as 1964 with a couple exceptions: Charcoal Moire was no longer offered and Red Stain was added, and Grey Ripple was changed to Black Ripple. The color printing of the catalog improved dramatically. The same colors were offered through the printing of the Chanute catalog.

CAMCO

gold lacquer kit circa 1973,
from the collection of Ben Goldberg

The 3D Moire pattern is almost always seen in white only. This finish is iridescent, changing as you view it from different angles.

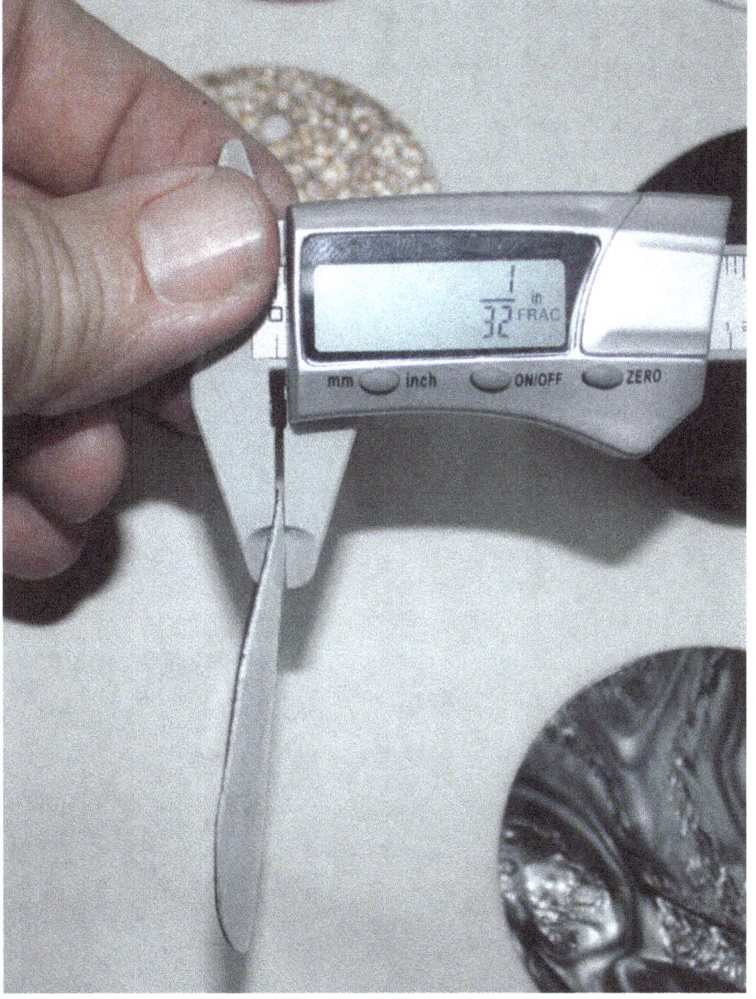

left: measuring a Moire finish sample at 1/32",
As was the case with other companies, the coverings that Camco used varied in thickness; the sparkle finishes were the thickest, usually about 3/64".

CAMCO

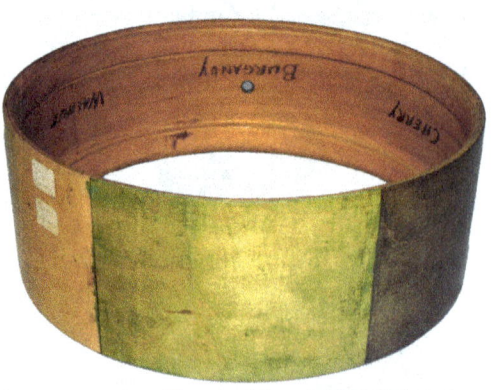

Camco sample lacquer shell from the collection of Drugan's Drums (Oak Lawn, Illinois, U.S.A. badge)
Colors, from left to right: Cherry, Burgundy, Walnut, Clear, Green Moss, Ebony

Natural Finish

Maple

Walnut

Stradivarius

Ebony

Lacquer Finish

White

Black

Alice Cooper Blue

Alice Cooper White

Covered Finish

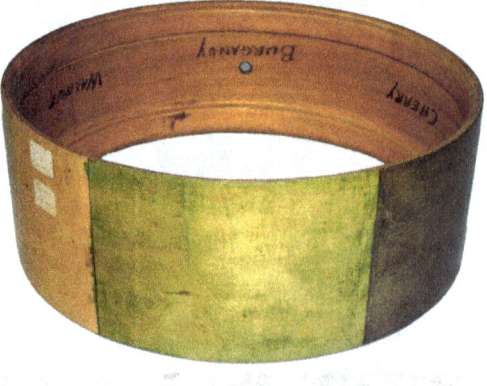
White Marine

Red

Blue

Black

1975 (Los Angeles) Color Swtch

CAMCO

CAMCO

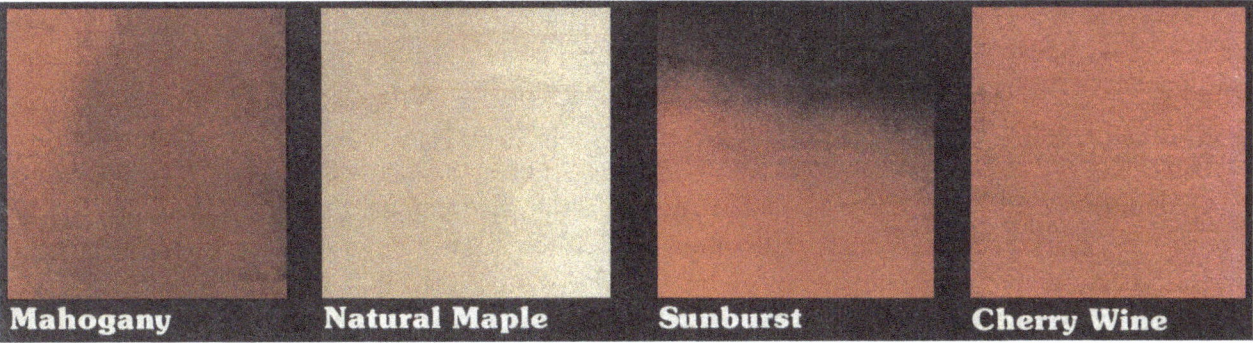

Mahogany | Natural Maple | Sunburst | Cherry Wine

1979 (Hoshino)
A typed note was included with the catalog: "Enclosed is the new Camco catalog showing you our latest offerings. For the time being, the sets showing in the catalog are available in Natural, Mahogany, Sunburst, and the amazing Natural Renaissance. Camco Renaissance drums are hand inlaid with a beautiful wood marquetry and finished in a gloss lacquer. No other drum company has ever attempted such a high level of hand craftsmanship and we suspect they never will."

Inset: Sunburst finish Hoshino-era Camco kit from the collection of Joe Luoma
Background: Hoshino-era Renaissance Series with hand-inlaid marquetry

FIBES

The Fibes company was formed in 1966 and built on the concept of fiberglass drums. Fibes was the first company to make a fiberglass drum covered with a chromed covering. The company was acquired by C.F. Martin in 1970. In their first Fibes catalog, Martin listed clear and colored (smoky or frosted) acrylic (Crystalite) drums and fiberglass drums covered with Antique Copper, Antique Brass, and Black or Sapphire Blue "Fivel", a flocked covered resembling velvet. The series of Fivel finishes was later expanded to include Peacock, Crimson Red, Pumpkin Orange, and blends. Martin's second Fibes catalog, of 1972, listed as new finishes chrome, black, white, and some rather unusual finishes: Agate (a marble laminate in browns and golds), Herblock (one of the first butcher block type finishes), and Buckskin, a covering with the look and feel of suede. A special run of transparent hot pink acrylic Fibes drums were produced exclusively for NYC's Sam Ash Music.

In 1979 Don Corder purchased the Fibes drum assets from C.F. Martin. The name Fibes was not included in the sale, as it was used to market a line of drumsticks. In 1990, Corder sold the "Fibes" assets to Ken Austin who started the Darwin Drum Company. The lugs used had the Fibes look, but the shells were wood and supplied in both lacquered and covered finishes. The promotional literature pictured drums in Deep Cherry, Dark Royal Blue, Black, and a White Marine Pearl. A Copper snare was also produced.

Tommy Robertson bought the company in 1995, and also managed to acquire rights to the Fibes name, bringing the name Fibes and the Fibes designs back together again. He continued making wood shell drums as well as fiberglass and acrylic snare drums. (Robertson used Jasper wood shells until be bought his own shell-making equipment.)

GRETSCH

As with other sections of the dating guide, the dates listed here are for the most part the dates these colors were listed in catalogs. Be advised that exceptions to these color dates abound. Rick Gier: *"Much internet forum discussion and many anecdotal comments put a rough range of availability of a finish three years before it appears and three years after it disappears from a catalog. This range may be even larger, depending upon the frequency of production of catalogs and the supply of particular finishes."*

There were often variations of these colors. Much like dyed fabrics that vary by dye lots, drum covering tints change from batch to batch.

In the case of sparkle finishes, they fluctuated between glass (glitter) and foil (sparkle). A common trend was for some colors to be glitter in the early 60s, change to sparkle, then later back to glitter again– all the while being catalogued as "sparkle;" Gretsch never referred to any covered finishes as glitter. Tangerine Sparkle was always glitter. Champagne Sparkle, Burgundy Sparkle, and Starlight Sparkle were always sparkle. Blue, gold, red, green, and silver varried between glitter and sparkle.

KMC is to be commended for naming their recent glass glitter colors in a manner that identifies them as glass glitter.

The thickness of the coverings varied greatly. The author has measured swatch samples that range from .005" (Black Nitron) to .021" (Tangerine Sparkle) with the latter being so thick that this factor alone can cause poor drum head fitting.

There are many reasons for the fluctuations described above, not the least of which is the fact that Gretsch was constantly shopping for more economical sources of supply and numerous vendors were used over the years.

USA GRETSCH

Color	Dates
Anniversary Sparkle	1958-1962
Antique Maple	1977-1979, 1982-2013
Aqua (Satin) Flame	1965-1972
Azure Gloss	2005-2013
Black Chrome Steel	1977-1978
Black Duco	2004-2013
Black Ebony / Ebony Gloss	1984-2013
Black Glass (Glitter)	2005-2013
Black Marine Pearl	2003-2013
Black ("Diamond") Pearl	1948-1978
(Jet) Black Nitron/Solid Black	1953-2013
Black Sparkle	1992-2013
Blue Duco	2004-2013
Blue Glass (Glitter)	2005-2013
Blue Metallic	1955-1958
Blue Nitron	1992-1999
Blue Oyster (Brooklyn Series)	2013
Blue Sparkle	1939-1978, 2003-2012
Blue Spruce	1977-1978, 1985-1986
Brass Steel	1972-1978
Bright Pink	1986-1990
Burgundy Sparkle	1962-1971
Burnt Orange	1983-2013
Cadillac Green (paint over plastic)	early 1950s-1959
(Steve Ferrone/'08 RB only)	2006-2013
Cameo Coral (paint over plastic)	1953-1959
Candy Red (lacquer)	1984
Caribbean Blue	1984-90, 2000, 2007-2013
Champagne Sparkle	1959-1976, 1993-2013
Chestnut Duco	2011-2013
Chinese Red & Ebony (lacquer) (Harlequin)	1955-1959
Chrome Nitron	1971
Chrome	1992-1999
Chrome Steel	1972-1978
Copper Metallic	1953-1958
Copper Mist (paint over plastic)	1953-1959
Cream Oyster (Brooklyn Series)	2012-2013
Curly Antique Maple Lacquer (125th Anniversary 5x14)	2008
Curly Walnut Maple Gloss	2007-2009
Curly Maple	2009-2013
Curly Millennium Maple Gloss	2005-2009
Curly Maple Rosewood Gloss	2006-2009
Curly Maple Stardust Gloss	2005-2009
Dark Red Nitron	1992-2003
Dark Walnut	1985-2013
Duco Ebony (aka "Full Dress Duco")	1939-1976
Duco White (aka "Full Dress Duco")	1939-1976
Ebony (lacquer)	1985-2013
Ebony (wood grain)	1977-1978
Emerald Green Pearl	1969-1972
Full Dress Duco (White or Ebony)	1939-1976
Gloss Vintage Blonde	2013
Gloss Classic Maple	2013
Gold Glass (Glitter)	2005-2013
Gold Mist Gloss	2005-2013
Gold Sparkle	1992-2013
Gold Nitron	1971-1972
Gold (Satin) Flame (130th Anniversary kits)	1965-1972 (2013)
Grand Piano Black	1986-1999, 2009-2013
Grand Piano White	1986-1999, 2009-2013
Green Metallic	1953-1958
Green Glass (Glitter)	2005-2013
Green Sparkle	1939-1976, 1992-2013
Grey Oyster (Brooklyn Series)	2012-2013
Harlequin (lacquer)	2009-2013
Hot Pink (lacquer)	1983-1986
Ice Blue (lacquer)	1984-1990
Jade Green Gloss	2006-2013
Jade Green Silk	1992-1999
Jet Black Nitron	1953-2013
Kool Green	1984-1986
Light Blue Nitron	1992-1997
Light Blue Pearl (snare only)	1999 only
Lucerne Green	1984-1990
Lustre-Blue Lacquer	1948-1953
Mahogany	1939-1976
Marine (White Pearl)	1950-1953
Metallic Gray	1992-2003
Midnight Blue Pearl	1948-1976
Millennium Maple (Natural)	2000-2013
Mirror Chrome	2003-2005
Mirror Gold	2003-2005

GRETSCH

Finish	Years
Moonglow Satin Flame	1968-1972
Natural Maple	1970-1999
Olive Satin Flame	1965-1969
Oyster White Pearl	1992-1999
Peacock (Satin) Flame	1970-1974
Peacock (Sparkle)	1955-1958
Pewter Sparkle (130th Brooklyn Kits only)	2013
Piano Black Gloss	2009-2013
Piano White Gloss	2009-2013
Pink Flame	1992-2001

Note: this is a reissue of the late 1960s "Sunset Flame"

Finish	Years
Plum Purple (lacquer)	1983-2013
Purple Glass (Glitter)	2005-2013
Red (lacquer)	1985-1990
Red Duco	2009-2013
Red Glass (Glitter)	2005-2013
Red Nitron	1993-1999
Red Oyster (Brooklyn Series)	2012-2013
Red Sparkle	1949-1978, 1992-2013
Red Rosewood	1972-2013
Red Wine Pearl	1969-1972
Salmon Satin Flame	see Sunset Satin Flame
Satin Azure Blue	2002-2013
Satin Burnt Orange	2000-2013
(Broadkaster / 1999-2003)	
Satin Caribbean Blue	2000, 2007-2013
Satin Cherry Red	2002-2005, 2008-2013
Satin Classic Maple	2009-2013
Satin Dark Ebony (Brooklyn Series)	2012-2013
Satin Dark Walnut	2005-2013
Satin Ebony	2000-2013
(Broadkaster / 1998-2005)	
Satin Emerald Green (Brooklyn Series)	2012-2013
Satin Mahogany (Brooklyn Series)	2012-2013
Satin Maple	2000-2009
(Broadkaster / 1999-2003)	
Satin Millennium Maple	2009-2013
Satin Natural (Brooklyn Series)	2013
Satin Purple	2005-2013
Satin Rosewood	2000-2013
(Broadkaster / 1998-2003)	
Satin Sable Black	2002-2005
Satin Sun Amber	2002-2013
Satin Tabasco	2009-2013
Satin Tabasco (Brooklyn Series)	2012-2013
Satin Vintage Blond	2002-2013
Satin Vintage Cherry Burst (130th Anniversary kits)	2013
Satin Walnut	2000-2013
(Broadkaster / 1998-2003)	
Savannah Sunset Duco	2011-2013
Silver Glass (Glitter)	2005-2013
Silver Mist (Lacquer) Gloss	2005-2013
Silver Sparkle	1939-78, '92-2001, '03-13
Silver Satin Flame (130th Anniversary sets)	1965-1968 (2013)
Simulated Rosewood	1977-1978
Sky Blue Pearl Nitron	1998-2013
Smoke Oriental Pearl	1939-1947
Solid Gretsch Orange	2009-2013
Sparkling Blue / Blue Sparkle	1939-1978, 2003-2013
Sparkling Gold/Gold Sparkle	1939-1978, 1992-2001, 2003-2013
Sparkling Green / Green Sparkle	1939-1976, 1992-2013
Sparkling Silver / Silver Sparkle	1939-1978, 1992-2013
Starlight Sparkle	1959-1962
Sun Amber Gloss	2005-2013
Sunset Satin Flame	1968-1970

Note: Sunset Flame was never illustrated in a catalog product photo or color swatch page. The only catalog that even mentioned it by name was the 1968 catalog. Collectors have been known to refer to this as Salmon Satin Flame. This color was reintroduced in 1992 as Pink Flame.

Finish	Years
Tangerine Sparkle	1962-1972, 2003-2013
Tri-Tone Blue & Silver (lacquer)	1939-1976, 2003
Tri-Tone Green & Silver (lacquer)	1961-1966
Tri-Tone Sparkles	1966-1976
(usually Blue & Gold or Red & Silver)	
Turquoise Glass (Glitter)	2005-2013
Turquoise Sparkle	2003-2013
Twilight Glass	2012-2013
Two-Tone/Tri-Tone Duco	1939-1976, 2003
Duco: Blue & Silver	
Duco: Blue & Gold (very rare)	
Duco: Red & Gold (very rare)	
Duco: Black & Gold	
Duco: Red & Silver (very rare)	
Duco: Black & Silver	2003
Metallic Lacquer: Green	1954
Metallic Lacquer: Copper	1954
Metallic Lacquer: Blue	1954
Metallic Lacquer: Red	1954
Two-Tone Baroque Pearl	1948
Two-Tone Catalina Green / Ivory (lacquer)	1955-1959
Two-Tone Charcoal Gray / Cameo Coral (lacquer)	1955-1959
Two-Tone Chinese Red / Metallic Gray (lacquer)	1958-1959
Vintage Champagne Sparkle	2006-2013
Vintage Marine (White Marine Pearl Yellowed)	2003-2013
Vintage Oyster White	2009-2013
(Tony Williams) Yellow Lacquer	1985-1995, 2003-2013
Yellow Nitron	1981-1990, 1996-1999
Walnut (Rich Walnut)	1968-2013
White Marine Nitron (White Marine Pearl)	2003-2013
White Marine Pearl	2000-2001
White Marine Pearl Nitron	2002-2003
White Nitron / Solid White	1977-2013
White Oriental Pearl	1939-1947
White Pearl	1948-1950, 1954-1978
White Tiger Stripe	1996-2001

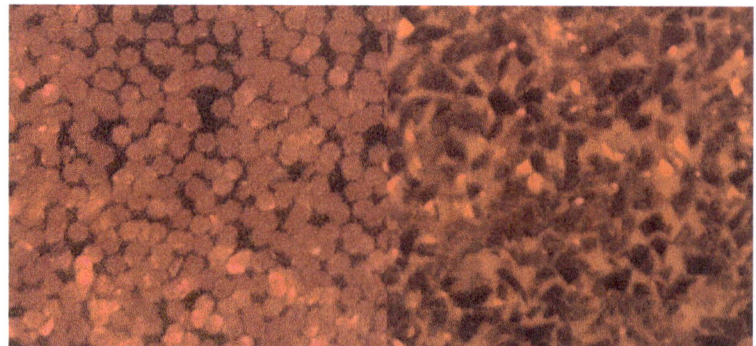

Sparkle (left) vs. Glitter (right)
Sparkle finishes were made with hex-shaped pieces of foil while glitters were made with actual shards of glass.

GRETSCH

COLOR CODES

In 1979, Gretsch began listing finish codes in their price lists, which corresponded to the codes on the drum labels. The codes listed for each year here represent colors that were new that year, not all colors available in that year. The codes used are as follows by year and alphabetically:

1979
NB – Jet Black Nitron
NW – White Nitron
WM – Natural Maple
WR – Red Rosewood
WW – Walnut
1981
NY – Yellow Nitron
1982
AM – Antique Maple
1983*
PR – Plum Purple
WO – Burnt Orange
PK – Hot Pink
1984
EB – Black Ebony
CB – Caribbean Blue
GR – Lucerne Green
1985
IB – Ice Blue
KG – Kool Green
BS – Blue Spruce
RD – Red
DKWW – Dark Walnut
TWYL – Tony Williams Yellow
1986
PB – Grand Piano Black
9/1986
PW – Grand Piano White
BP – Bright Pink
1992
AUSP – Gold Sparkle
GSP – Green Sparkle
DRN – Dark Red Nitron
LBP – Light Blue Nitron
JGF – Jade Green Silk
C – Chrome
BKSP – Black Sparkle
RSP – Red Sparkle
CSP – Champagne Sparkle
BN – Blue Nitron
RN – Red Nitron
OWP – Oyster White Pearl
PF – Pink Flame
MG – Metallic Grey
SSP – Silver Sparkle
2000
GMM – Millennium Maple (Natural)
SWW – Satin Walnut
SWM – Satin Maple
SWO – Satin Burnt Orange
SWR – Satin Rosewood
SEB – Satin Ebony
SCB – Satin Caribbean Blue (2000 only)
GWMP – White Marine Pearl Nitron
SBP – Sky Blue Pearl Nitron
2002
ABO – Satin Azure Blue
CRO – Satin Cherry Red (discontinued '05)
VBO – Satin Vintage Blond
SAO – Satin Sun Amber
SBO – Satin Sable Black (discontinued '05)
2003
TGSP – Tangerine Sparkle
TQSP – Turquoise Sparkle
BLSP – Blue Sparkle
VMP – Vintage Marine
BMP – Black Marine
MC – Mirror Chrome
MG – Mirror Gold
WMP – White Marine Nitron
2004
BL – Blue Duco
BK – Black Duco
2005
ABG – Azure Gloss
SAG – Sun Amber Gloss
SMG – Silver Mist Gloss
GMG – Gold Mist Gloss
SPR – Satin Purple
SDKW – Satin Dark Walnut
AUGP – Gold Glass (Glitter)
BLGP – Blue Glass (Glitter)
RGP – Red Glass (Glitter)
GGP - Green Glass (Glitter)
SGP - Silver Glass (Glitter)
BKGP - Black Glass (Glitter)
TQGP - Turquoise Glass (Glitter)
PGP - Purple Glass (Glitter)
CMM – Curly Millennium Gloss
CSD – Curly Stardust Maple Gloss
2006
VCS – Vintage Champagne Sparkle
JG – Jade Green Gloss
CG – 1955 Cadillac Green (Steve Ferrone signature series only)
CWR – Curly Rosewood Maple Gloss
2007
SCB – Caribbean Blue (Satin)
CB – Caribbean Blue
CWW – Curly Walnut Maple Gloss
2008
AM -- Curly Antique Maple Lacquer (125th Anniversary 5x14 only)
CRO – Satin Cherry Red
2009
PWG – Piano White Gloss
PBG – Piano Black Gloss
GOG – Solid Gretsch Orange
SCM – Satin Classic Maple
CM – Curly Maple
STB – Satin Tabasco
HQ – Harlequin (lacquer) (add any finish code)
SN – Satin Natural (New Classic)
VOW – Vintage Oyster White
RD – Red Duco
2011
SAV – Savannah Sunset Duco
CST – Chestnut Duco
2012
TWGP – Twilight Glass
SDE – Dark Ebony (Brooklyn Series)
SEG – Emerald Green (Brooklyn Series)
SM – Mahogany (Brooklyn Series)
ST – Tabasco (Brooklyn Series)
CO – Cream Oyster (Brooklyn Series)
GO – Grey Oyster (Brooklyn Series)
RO – Red Oyster (Brooklyn Series)
BO – Blue Oyster (Brooklyn Series)
*There are no codes for the Centennial finishes – "Birdseye Maple," "Carpathian Elm" and "Burl Walnut" – or 1980s Blackhawk finishes – "Black," "Silver", "Dark Blue", "White", "Burgundy" "Metallics", "Gun Metal Blue", & "Candy Apple Red".

IMPORT COLORS

New Classic Series
BSL – Black Sparkle Lacquer	2011-2013
DC – Deep Cherry Gloss	2006-2008
IMP – Ivory Marine Pearl	2007-2013
MS – Merlot Sparkle	2008-2010
OSB – Ocean Sparkle Burst	2010-2013
SN – Satin Natural	2009-2013
SM – Silver Metallic	2013
VG – Vintage Glass Nitron	2006-2013

Renown Maple Series
BL – Deep Blue Lacquer	2001-2005
BK – Deep Black Lacquer	2001-2003
RD – Deep Red Lacquer	2001-2003
DA – Deep Amber Lacquer	2002-2005
CB – Cherry Burst	2002-2013
CS – Champagne Silk	2002-2006
AB – Autumn Burst	2003-2012
RC – Red Cherry	2003-2006
MP – Magenta Purple	2003-2006
PB – Piano Black	2003-2006
BB – Blue Burst	2006-2008
SL – Slate Silver Sparkle	2006-2010
DIGS – Deep Inca Gold Sparkle	2008-2010
SB – Satin Black	2010-2013
RSF – Ruby Sparkle Fade	2010-2012
CSF – Cobalt Sparkle Fade	2011-2012
MCB – Motor City Blue (Renown '57)	2011-2012
MCO- Motor City Onyx (Renown 57)	2011-2012
MCR- Motor City Red (Renown '57)	2012
MG - Midnight (Blue) Glass Glitter (only 25 kits)	2012
SW - Satin White	2013
GN - Gloss Natural	2013
SPO - Silver Oyster Pearl	2013
BM - Blue Metal	2013

Catalina Elite
DW – Dark Walnut Lacquer	2001-2003
SB – Smoky Black Lacquer	2001-2003
RR – Ruby Red Lacquer	2001-2003

Catalina Stage
SF – Silver Frost	2001-2003
BK – Liquid Black	2001-2003
WR – Wine Red	2001-2003

Catalina Birch
VB – Vintage Burst	2003-2006
CB – Caribbean Blue	2003-2007
RC – Red Cherry	2003-2006
DW – Dark Walnut	2003-2007
CF – Chestnut Fade	2005-2007
WB – Walnut Burst	2010-2012
CBB – Cobalt Blue Burst	2010-2012
WP – White Pearl	2010-2011
SS – Silver Sparkle	2010-2011
EDHB – Ebony Diamond Halogen Burst	2011-2012
BDHF – Blue Diamond Halogen Fade	2011-2012
SC – Satin Cherry	2011-2012
SW - Satin Walnut	2012 only

Catalina Club
WP – White Marine (Pearl)	2003-2013
BP – Black Marine (Pearl)	2003-2006
SS – Silver Sparkle	2003-2008
OS – Onyx Silver	2004-2005
SN – Satin Natural	2008-2013
RSP – Rustic Pearl	2008-2010
RBD – Royal Blue Diamond	2009

GRETSCH

BP – 1964 Reissue Black Pearl
 (Guitar Center only) 2008-2009
WG – Walnut Glaze 2009-2013
EGF – Emerald Green Flake 2010-2011
COS – Copper Sparkle 2010-2013
GN – Gloss Natural 2010-2013
WKP – Whiskey Pearl 2011
WMG –White Mint Green Fade Pearl 2011
GBS – Galaxy Black Sparkle 2011-2013
TS–Teal Sparkle (same as Turquoise Sparkle) 2012
Catalina Club Mod
BA – Blue Alien 2006-2008
BS – Black over Silver Sparkle Stripe
 2006-2009
SB – Silver Stripe over Black Sparkle
 2007-2008
TAT – Tattoo 2008-2010
GT – G-Tube 2009-2010
Catalina Club Mini Mod
BW – Black Widow 2008-2010
YJ – Yellow Jacket 2009-2010
Catalina Club Rock
BF – Black Flake UV Gloss 2006-2008
SS – Silver Sparkle 2006-2008
SS – Silver Sparkle over Silver Lacquer
 2008-2009
SB – Silver Sparkle over Black Lacquer
 2008-2010
GE – Gloss Ebony 2010-2013

OT - Ocean Twilight 2013
MC - Mirror Chrome 2013
COS - Copper Sparkle 2013
GBS - Galaxy Black Sparkle 2013
Catalina Club Classic
OT - Ocean Twilight 2013
COS - Copper Sparkle 2013
GBS - Galaxy Black Sparkle 2013
Catalina Club Street
TSS - Silver Sparkle 2013
TRS - Red Sparkle 2013
Catalina Maple
MR – Cherry Red 2006-10/1/10
MA – Deep Amber 2006-10/1/10
TFS –Tobacco Fade Sunburst
 2007-10/1/10
EBB–Ebony, Black Hardware
 2009-10/1/10
MOF–Mocha Fade
 1/1/10-10/1/10, 2011-13
AMB – Amber 10/1/10-2013
CG – Cherry Gloss 10/1/10-2013
TE – Transparent Ebony 10/1/10-2013
DCB – Dark Cherry Burst 2011-2013
SWF – Satin Walnut Fade 2013
Catalina Ash
AR – Deep Red 2006-2010
AC – Cobalt Blue (UV gloss) 2006-10/1/10
LBB – Liquid Black (Wrap) 2008-10/1/10

BCF – Black Cherry Fade (UV gloss)
 2010-10/1/10
Blackhawk
Black Metallic 1983-1988
Dark Blue Metallic 1983-1988
Silver Metallic 1983-1990
Burgundy Metallic 1985-1988
White Metallic 1986-1990
Candy Apple Red 1989-1990
Gun Metal Blue 1989-1990
LB – Liquid Black 2003-2011
WR – Wine Red 2003-2011
BM – Blue Metallic 2003-2007
BS – Blue Oyster Swirl 2004-2007
ES – Ebony Oyster Swirl 2004-2007
WD – White Diamond 2005-2007
BD – Blue Diamond 2005-2007
ED -- Ebony Diamond 2005-2007
MLB – Metallic Liquid Blue 2008-2011
Energy Series
BLK – Black 2012-2013
GST – Grey Steel 2012-2013
WHT – White 2012-2013
Renegade Series
BLK – Black 2012-2013
SIL – Silver 2012-2013
WR – Wine Red 2012-2013

DIXIELAND SEPARATE TENSION SNARE DRUM
(Shell size 14"x5½".) Top value in a snappy, modern orchestra snare drum at a mighty low price. The shell is the GRETSCH-Exclusive 3-ply moulded, perfect-round, guaranteed for the life of the drum! Single flanged non-rusting hoops; streamlined tension rod casings; Standard throw-off snare strainer with snare bracket; 12-strand "Responso" all-metal snares. Metal parts polished CHROME PLATED. Prices include tax.
X4104—Dixieland Snare Drum, Red, Copper, Green or Blue metallic lacquer and chrome. .... Ea. $48.00
X4105—Dixieland Snare Drum, Gretsch-Pearl Finish, Chrome Plated Metal Parts. ....Ea. 52.00

The Dixieland snare drum was offered in some unique finishes: Copper, Green, and Blue metallic lacquer. The lacquer was applied directly to the wood. These Green and Copper shells have been mistaken for Cadillac Green and Copper Mist which, along with Cameo Coral, were lacquer applied to clear covering; buyer beware!

Cadillac Green, Copper Mist, and Cameo Coral were lacquer finishes applied to clear pyralin wrap. Some, but not all, drums with this treatment appear to have some type of mesh under the clear pyralin as illustrated here. (see page 208)

Gretsch began to call these finishes "Nitron" finishes in the 1950s. Gretsch used the "Nitron" term on solid-color tinted pyralin coverings through the 1970s, 1980s, and 1990s.

GRETSCH

Translucent Pearl Covering
Both the kit here as well as early examples of Midnight Blue were created by applying lacquer (Duco, or dual-color) to the shells, then applying a translucent covering with the design embedded in it.

1958

| Peacock Sparkle | Green Sparkle | Gold Sparkle | Blue Sparkle | Silver Sparkle | Red Sparkle |

| Copper Mist | Cadillac Green | Cameo Coral | Midnight Blue | Black Pearl | White Pearl |

GRETSCH
1961 (Catalog #40)

GOLD SPARKLE PEARL

BLUE SPARKLE PEARL

MIDNIGHT BLUE PEARL
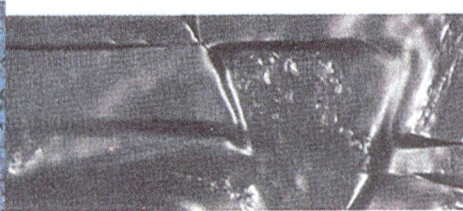

ANNIVERSARY SPARKLE PEARL
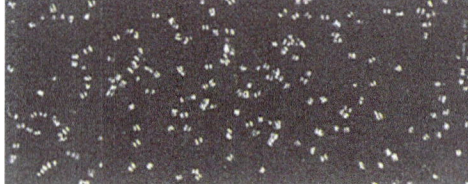

SILVER SPARKLE PEARL
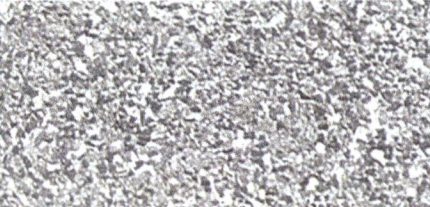

BLACK PEARL

WHITE PEARL

RED SPARKLE PEARL

JET BLACK

CHAMPAGNE SPARKLE PEARL

GREEN SPARKLE PEARL
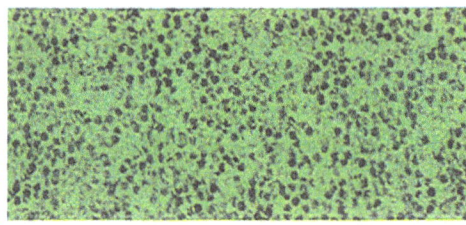

STARLIGHT SPARKLE PEARL

Lee Ruff comment on Champagne Sparkle vs Peacock Sparkle: "The grain in both finishes was very fine, and from a few feet away, they looked almost identical. My first new Gretsch set was Champagne Sparkle, and Gretsch said it was one of the 1st in Champagne. I ordered it in 1960 at Mars Music Store in Elkton, MD. The Peacock Sparkle had "tiny" grains in red, green, and gold. Over the years, many Peacock Sparkle drums have been mistaken for Champagne. Under the lights, the finishes were practically indiscernible. Champagne was made with a unique process. Particles of copper were actually used. Peacock Sparkle was made the same way, using colored particles under clear. The other sparkles and/or glitters were made of silver particles with a tinted translucent layer over top. "Moderately faded" Peacock Sparkle today looks almost identical to Champagne at close scrutiny."

Catalog #42 of 1963: Same colors as above with the exception of Anniversary Sparkle Pearl and Starlight Sparkle Pearl, which were replaced by Tangerine and Burgundy Sparkles below

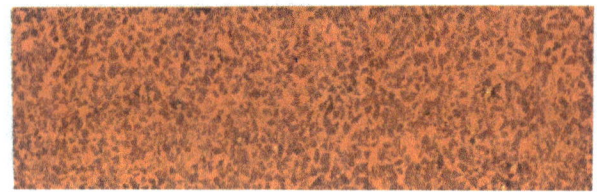

GRETSCH
1966

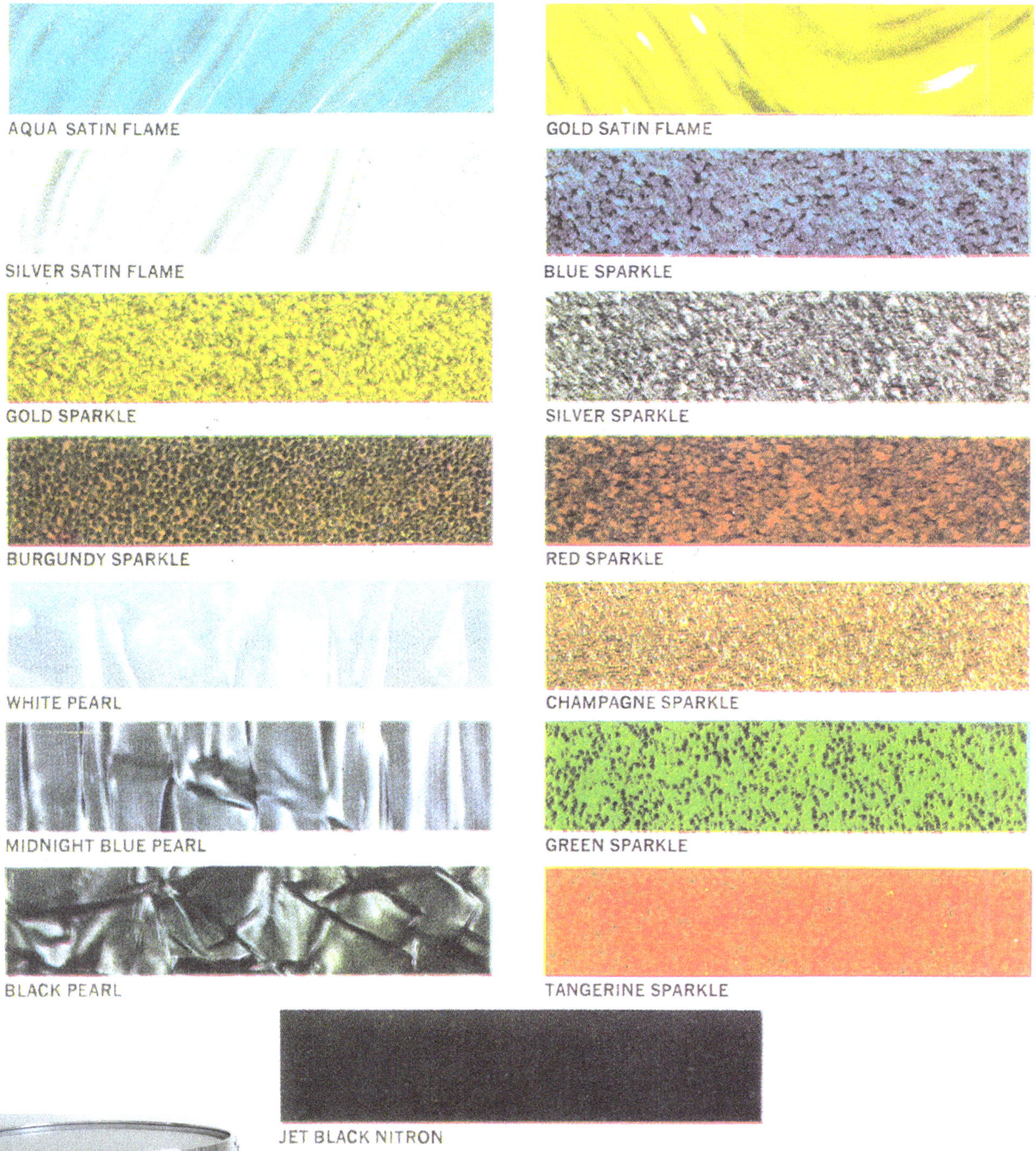

AQUA SATIN FLAME	GOLD SATIN FLAME
SILVER SATIN FLAME	BLUE SPARKLE
GOLD SPARKLE	SILVER SPARKLE
BURGUNDY SPARKLE	RED SPARKLE
WHITE PEARL	CHAMPAGNE SPARKLE
MIDNIGHT BLUE PEARL	GREEN SPARKLE
BLACK PEARL	TANGERINE SPARKLE

JET BLACK NITRON

The snare drum photo at right is from the 2006 *Gretsch News*, presented then as a limited edition (one of 50 drums) of Jade Green Silk. This finish was a standard color from 1992 to 1999. A very similar color was produced briefly in the mid-to-late-1960s (floor tom pictured at left is from 1969) but never catalogued or swatched. Our color list includes it as Olive Satin Flame.

GRETSCH
1971 & 1973

THE GREAT GRETSCH COLORS

GLEAMING GRETSCH PEARLS, SPARKLES AND SATIN FLAMES — on the bandstand or on parade the choice of America's top drummers.

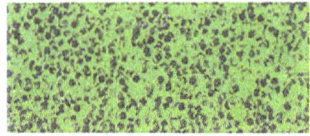
GREEN SPARKLE

AQUA FLAME

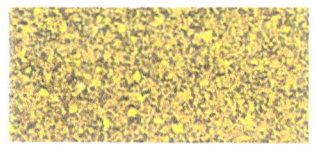
GOLD SPARKLE

TANGERINE SPARKLE

GOLD FLAME

RED SPARKLE

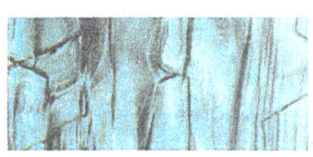
WHITE PEARL

MOONGLOW FLAME

SILVER SPARKLE

EMERALD GREEN PEARL

PEACOCK FLAME

BLUE SPARKLE

MIDNIGHT BLUE PEARL

CHROME NITRON

BURGUNDY SPARKLE

RED WINE PEARL

JET BLACK NITRON

CHAMPAGNE SPARKLE

BLACK PEARL

GOLD NITRON

GRETSCH

GRETSCH
1977

Wood Finishes: Ebony, Blue Spruce, Antique Maple, Red Rosewood, Natural Maple, Walnut, Simulated Rosewood

Pearl Finishes: Sparkle Silver, Jet Black Nitron, Sparkle Blue, White Nitron, Sparkle Gold, Black Pearl, White Pearl

Metal Finishes: Chrome Steel, Black Chrome Steel

New lacquer finishes, 1984: Kool Green, Candy Red, Ice Blue
Introduced as Candy Red, by the time the next price list was published, the name was shortened to Red.

GRETSCH
Gretsch after 1977

No Gretsch drum catalogs were published after 1980 until the 1983 poster-format catalog. That poster had some color swatches, but the tiny slivers of color would serve no useful purpose here. Three new and rather unusual finishes of 1983 were Burnt Orange, Plum Purple, and Hot Pink. The other finishes offered at the time were Natural Maple, Antique Maple, Jet Black Nitron, White Nitron, Walnut, Red Rosewood, and Yellow Nitron. (The Nitron finishes are pearl coverings.)

The author is certain some of these Gretsch colors never appeared in Gretsch catalog color swatch form. This assortment of actual pearl samples is from the 1990s.

GRETSCH
Custom/Limited edition finishes

Model GCS-4177SS - 2007 only: Custom Series Square Snare Drum
5x14 USA Custom snare drum with 10 individual square color panels representing the most popular lacquer finishes: Antique Maple, Rosewood, Dark Walnut, Millennium Maple, Purple, Walnut, Azure Blue, Sun Amber, Ebony, Burnt Orange

Steve Maxwell Vintage and Custom Drums special finishes

Mardi Gras The recreation of this finish was accomplished through Steve working with the folks at KMC Music. In January of 2009 Steve and the folks at KMC had their first discussion about this issue. KMC had a desire to re-introduce a vintage finish from the past, and it didn't necessarily have to be a finish that was traditionally associated with Gretsch. Mardi Gras immediately came to Steve's mind and KMC agreed, so the plan was set in motion. There were different versions of Mardi Gras and they varied by drum manufacturer. Slingerland, Leedy and Rogers all had this finish, and each had a slightly different variation of it. Steve provided a pristine example of one of the original Mardi Gras versions and several prototypes of the finish were completed. The intent for the final product was to replicate the concept of the original Mardi Gras finish but with enough subtle differences so as to give this version its own unique character. The final version was approved March 13th, 2010 after almost 15 months of work, and the finish went into production.

Fiesta Pearl (left) is very similar to Mardi Gras, but with a white background instead of black. Maxwell has found combinations of the two finishes very popular; example at right.

Copper Mist
Very similar to the Copper Mist Nitron offered by Gretsch 1953-1959. Maxwell's tint is very similar, but is essentially a stain on the wood. It is offered as a gloss lacquer or a satin finish.

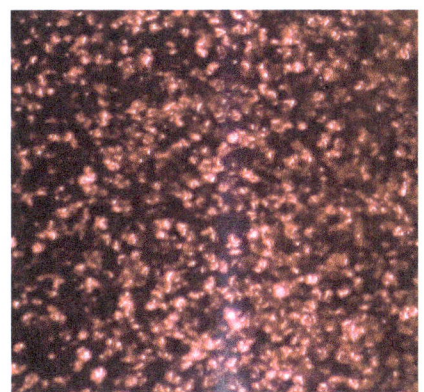

Merlot Sparkle
A close approximation of the vintage Burgundy Sparkle finish.
(Available on the New Classic Series from 2008-2010.)

Espresso Burst
A reproduction of the finish seen on page 109.

GRETSCH

July, 2011 USA Custom Finishes

Nitron Covered Finishes Finish Code "NIT"

 Blue Glass - BLGP
 Blue Sparkle - BLSP
 Champagne Sparkle - CS

 Gold Glass - AUGP
 Gold Sparkle - AUSP
 Green Glass - GGP
 Green Sparkle - GSP
Red Glass - RGP
Red Sparkle - RSP

 Silver Glass - SGP
 Silver Sparkle - SSP
 Sky Blue Pearl - SBP
 Solid Black - NB
 Solid White - NW
 Tangerine Glass - TGGP

Tangerine Sparkle - TGSP
 Turquoise Glass - TPGP
 Turquoise Sparkle - TQSP
 Twilight Glass - TWGP
White Marine Pearl - WMP
Vintage Marine Pearl - VMP

 Vintage Oyster White - VOW
 Vintage Champagne Sparkle - VCS
 Black Glass - BKGP
 Black Sparkle - BKSP
Black Marine Pearl - BMP
Purple Glass PGP (Not pictured)

Nitrocellulose Gloss Lacquer Finishes Finish Code "SPL"

Antique Maple - AM | Azure - ABG | Black Duco - BK |  Blue Duco - BL |  Burnt Orange - WO | 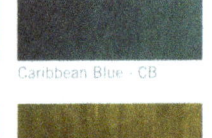 Caribbean Blue - CB

 Chestnut Duco - CST
 Dark Walnut - DKWN
 Ebony - EB
 Gold Mist - GMG
 Gretsch Orange - GOG
 Jade Green - JG

 Millennium Maple - GMM
 Piano Black - PBG
 Piano White - PWG
 Purple - PR
 Red Duco - RD
Rosewood - WR

Savannah Sunset Duco - SAV
 Silver Mist - SMG
 Solid Yellow - TWYL
Sun Amber - SAG
Walnut - WW

Nitrocellulose Lacquer Satin Finishes Finish Code "SAT"

 Satin Azure Blue - ABO
 Satin Burnt Orange - SWO
 Satin Classic Maple - SCM
 Satin Dark Walnut - SDKW
 Satin Ebony - SEB
 Satin Millennium Maple - SWM

Satin Purple - SPR | Satin Rosewood - SWR | Satin Sun Amber - SAO | Satin Tabasco - STB | Satin Vintage Blond - VBO | Satin Walnut - SWW

Satin Caribbean Blue - SCB (Not pictured), Satin Cherry Red - CRO (Not pictured)

Curly Maple Finishes Finish Code "CM"

Curly Maple features an outer ply of figured curly maple that adds a distinctive appearance to any drum. All Nitro Cellulose finishes (gloss, satin, Harlequin) are available in Curly Maple. See size chart for available sizes. Indicate "CM" for Curly Maple Finish.

Harlequin Finishes Finish Code "HQ"

     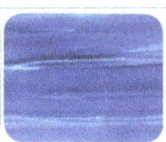  

Satin Mahogany | Satin Dark Ebony | Satin Tobasco | Satin Emerald | Grey Oyster | Blue Oyster | Cream Oyster | Red Oyster

LEEDY

For better than two decades, Leedy drums were only available in natural finishes of Walnut, Maple, and Mahogany. In about 1924 metal-shell drums were offered in black or white enamel and in 1925 these finishes were also offered on wood shell drums.

George Way is credited with being the first to wrap drums, in the 1920s. According to Way, the first kit to be wrapped was for Leedy endorser Chauncey Morehouse who was at the time playing with the Goldkette orchestra at the Greystoke Ballroom in Detroit. This first wraps were referred to in Leedy Literature as "American Pyroxylin", and by 1927 as "Dupont Pyralin." In 1941 there were "Dupont Pearl" and "Dupont plastic" finishes. The "Pearl" finishes refer to the designs in the Pyralin covering while the plastic was a less expensive but more fragile covering than Pyralin. For the first few years that covered drums were offered, the various finishes were presented as separate models.

Full-color printing was first used by Leedy in about 1925 when the illustration at right of Colonial Gold (a satin finish presented here with Nobby Gold hardware) appeared in a multi-page flier. Catalog O of 1927 used the illustration at left for Colonial Gold.

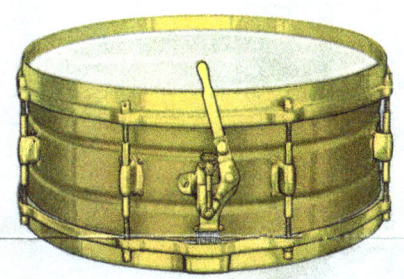

From the Curotto Collection:
Leedy Professional Model, in Colonial Gold, a Duco finish, 1927, with knobby gold hardware. This finish was originally made especially for Geo. W. Marsh, the Paul Whiteman drummer.

From the Curotto Collection:
uncatalogued "wallpaper" covering

A 20s Professional (left) and Utility, both from the Curotto Collection, in a non-catalogued "Stipel" finish. This finish is a heavily textured coating very similar to Ludwig's "Stipel Gold" of the same era (1926), but with a more reddish hue.

LEEDY

The first Leedy catalog to include color images of drums was 1927's Catalog O. A few full-color leaflets were published prior to that, like this 1925 introduction of of the Red and Black Onyx and Rainbow Pearl.
This 3.25" x 6.25" leaflet unfolded to 9.75" x 12.5"

Black Onyx (above),
Rainbow Pearl (right),
and Red Onyx (above right)
from The Curotto Collection

LEEDY

from the Curotto collection uncatalogued Green Onyx

Another version of Black Onyx, 1930
from the Curotto Collection

Sparkling Gold 1927-1965

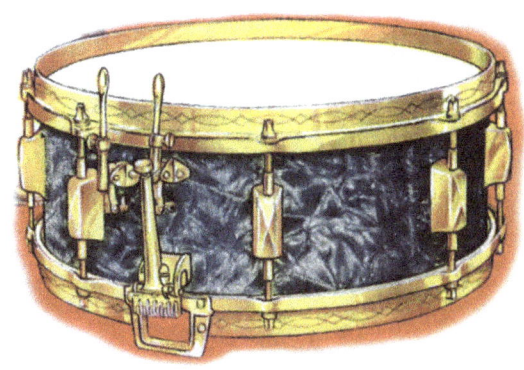

Black Pearl 1928-1965

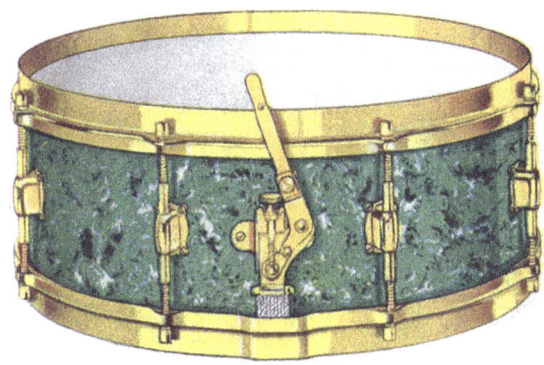

Jade Green 1927

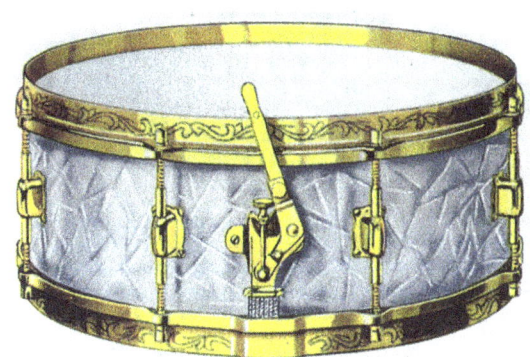

Marine Pearl 1927-1965

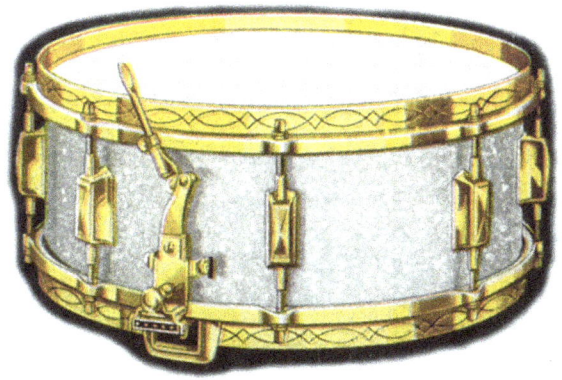

Sparkling Silver 1933-1965

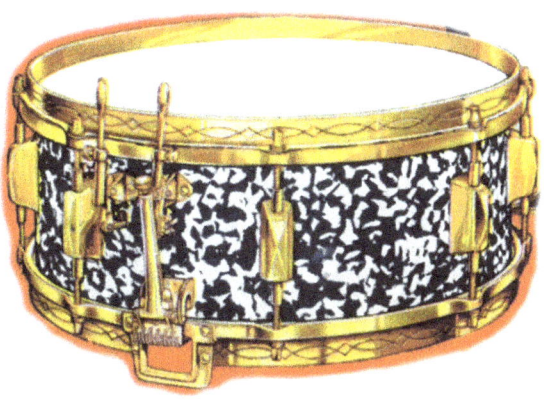

Black Onyx 1925-1928

LEEDY

Rainbow Pearl 1925-1930

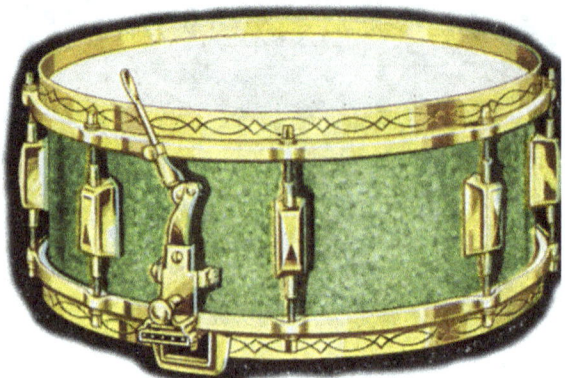

Sparkling Green 1933-1965

Green Pearl 1928

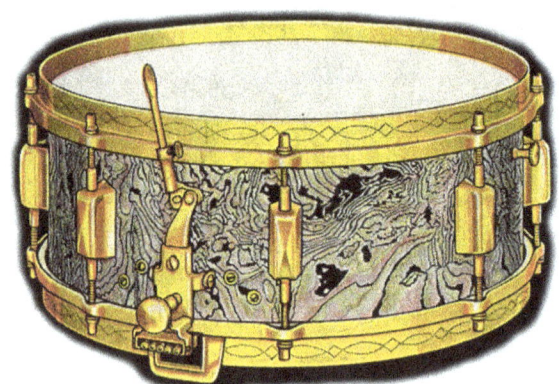

Oriental Pearl 1934-1936

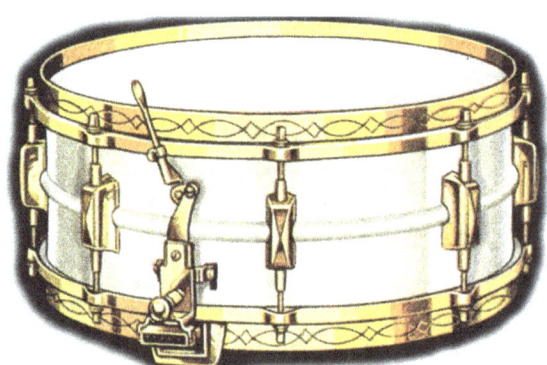

White Elite 1928-1935
White Duco with Nobby Gold hardware

Blue Tri-Tone Finish new 1934
Black and Gold lacquer added in 1940

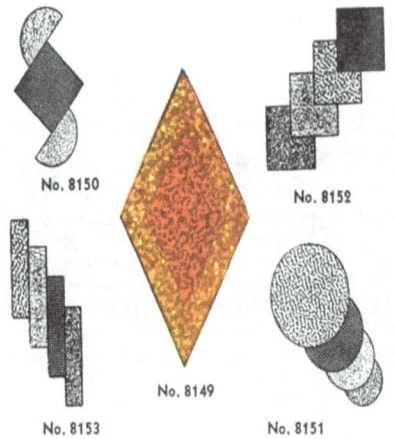

No. 8150   No. 8152
No. 8149
No. 8153   No. 8151

"Full Dress" Pearl Appliques
1933-1941

LEEDY

LEEDY

From The Curotto Collection

Sparkling Gold

Rainbow Pearl

Marine Pearl

LEEDY

Catalog 46 (1942)
Black/Gold and Blue/Silver were standard options beginning in about 1934.
Cream/Gold and Maroon/Gold were added in 1941.

Blue and Silver Lacquer from the Curotto Collection

Zebra finish, (uncatalogued) early 1950s from the Curotto Collection

Leedy and Dupont tried a plastic covering that was less expensive than pyralin in 1942. It was offered in only one color, Marine Green, and only on the "Challenger" outfit. The 1942 catalog image was in black and white, but a color leaflet featuring the finish and outfit was released.

LEEDY

**Autographs of the Stars
1942-1946**

Autographs of the Stars is one of the rarest Leedy finishes. The names of 212 Leedy endorsers were lithographed onto the underside of the clear pyralin that was laminated to the blue-green background material with the star pattern.

From the early 1990s to around 2005, only one complete outfit in this finish was known to exist and it was valued at about $15,000.00. Since then a couple more outfits have surfaced, but this remains one of Leedy's rarest finishes.

Autographs of the Stars was catalogued from 1942 to 1946, but examples of this finish are documented from 1941-1951. Mike Curotto's Leedy & Ludwig below is one such example from the early 1950s.

from the Curotto Collection

LEEDY
Rare Autographs of the Stars kit

At this writing, this outfit is the rarest and probably the most valuable vintage kit in existence with the exception of drums with celebrity attachment. Every other Autographs of the Stars kit is made with the blue-green background with stars; this kit was made with a white pearl background.

The original owner ordered the kit in 1941. When he passed away, Steve Maxwell brokered the sale of this kit to collector Mike Leshkevich in 2011. Mike Curotto purchased the outfit with the assistance of collector Tony Lewis in 2017.

The set includes a 4x10 tom with tacked top and bottom heads, 7x11 tom with tunable top and tacked bottom, 9x13 tom with tunable top and tacked bottom, 14x28 single tension bass drum, and 7x14 snare drum. All of the original hardware is present including the snare stand, foot pedal, high hat stand, rail for the bass drum along with both cymbal arms that attach to the rail. The tom holders for the 3 toms attach to the rail and are still with the kit.

LEEDY

Black Beauty Pearl 1962-1965	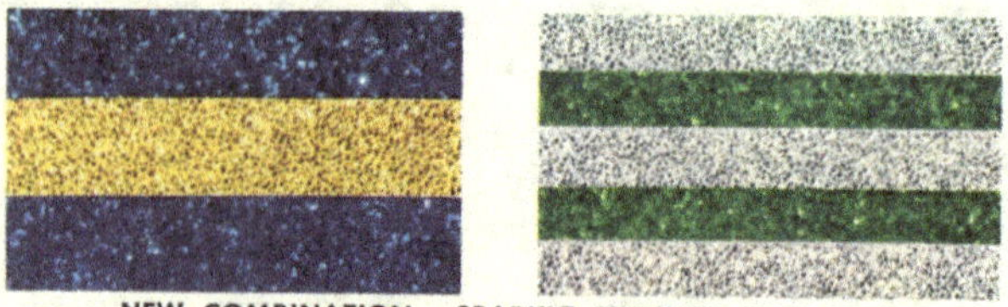 NEW COMBINATION – SPARKLE FINISHES AVAILABLE IN ANY TWO OF THE SEVEN SPARKLE PEARLS		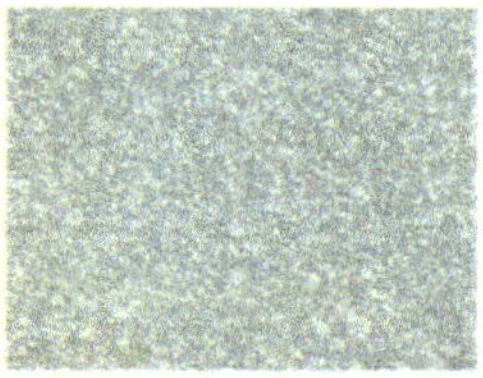 Aqua Sparkle Pearl 1960
 Blue Agate Pearl 1965	 Gray Agate Pearl 1965	 Light Blue Pearl 1960-1965	 Oyster Pink Pearl 1965
Blue Ripple Pearl 1965	 Red Ripple Pearl 1965	 Champagne Sparkle Pearl 1965	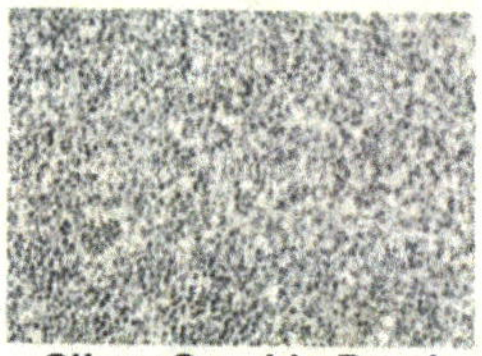 Silver Sparkle Pearl 1960-1965
Pink Sparkle Pearl 1960-1962	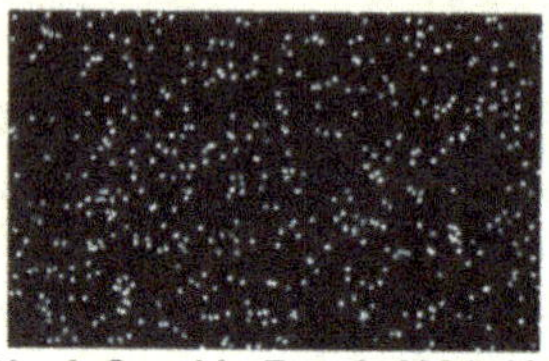 Black Sparkle Pearl 1960-1965	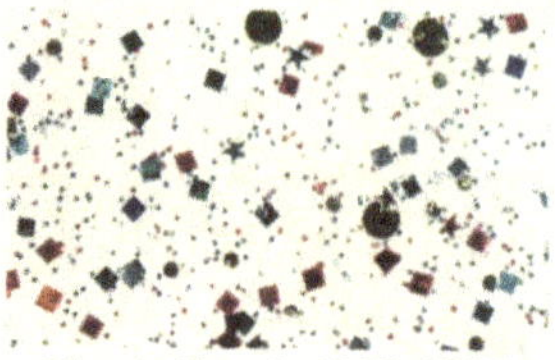 Fiesta Pearl 1960-1965	 White Satin Flame Pearl 1965
 Red Satin Flame Pearl 1965	 Blue Satin Flame Pearl 1965	Gold Satin Flame Pearl 1965	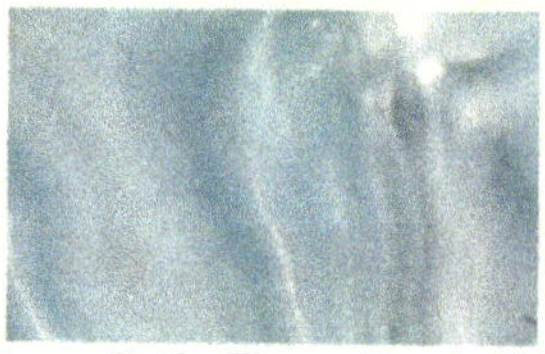 Green Satin Flame Pearl 1965

2003 limited edition   Gretsch-Leedy
From the Curotto Collection, "Hawaiian Shirt" or "Guitar Pick" finish.
This covering material was from the same batch that Slingerland used on a very limited number of drums.

LUDWIG COLORS*

Color	Years
Abalone Pearl	1936–1938
African Satinwood	1994–
Arctic (high-gloss lacquer)	1992–
Avalon Pearl	see White Marine Pearl
Birdseye Maple	1912–1914
Black Avalon Pearl	see Black Diamond Pearl
Black Cortex	1974–1984
Black Diamond Pearl	1936–1992, 1995–
Black (Pearl)	1978–
(from 1978–1993 known as Black Cortex)	
Black Ebonized	1925–1939
Black Gold	1998–
Black Gloss	1982–
Black Lacquer (WFL)	1938–1955
Black Oyster Pearl	1995–
(see also Oyster Black Pearl)	
Black Panther	1971–1975
Black Sparkle	1995–
Blue Frost Classic-coat	1992–1993
Blue (Pearl)	1994–
Blue Cortex	1978–1984
Blue Shadow	1992–1998
Blue Silk	1973–1984
Blue Sparkle	1947–1984
	1997–
Brushed Gold	1982–
Brushed Silver	1982–
Burgandy, Sparkling	1967
Butcher Block Cortex	1974–1984
Champagne Sparkle	1995–
(see also Pink Champagne)	
Charcoal Shadow	1992–
CherryStain	1993–
Chrome Pearl	1984-1995
Chrome-O-Wood	1978–1984
Citrus Mod	1971
Coral Stain	1998–
Crimson Classic Coat	1992–1993
Crystal	1941
Deluxe Marble (WFL)	1941
Emerald Green	1928–1930
Emerald Shadow	1994–
Flame Shadow	1994–1998
Galaxy	1962–1963
Gold Shadow	1998–
Gold, Brushed	1984
Gold Sparkle	1929–1984
Gold Silk	1973–1974
Green Sparkle	1932–1984
Lavender Pearl	1928–1935
Ludwigold	1927–1930
Mahogany	1912–1994
Mahogany Cortex	1973–1982
Maple, snare drums	1919–
Maple, outfits	1971–
Marble Cortex	1972–1978
Marble Pearl	1928–1929
Marble Lacquer (WFL)	1941
Marble Lacquers (Black, Ivory, Blue)	1994–1997
Mod Orange	1971
Multi-Color Lacquer	1934–1968
Multi-Color Lacquer (WFL)c	
Blue & Silver	1939–1955
Black & Gold	1939–1955
Blue & Gold	1939–1940
Oyster Black Pearl	1959–1975
Natural Red Mahogany	1982–
(see also Black Oyster Pearl)	
Oyster Blue Pearl	1959–1978
Oyster Pink Pearl	1959
Peacock Pearl I	1928–1930
Peacock Pearl II	1930–1932
Pink Campagne Pearl	1962–1975
Plum	1998–
Psychedelic Red	1971–1975
	2001–
Purple Shadow	1992–
Purple Sparkle	1997–
Rainbow Pearl: not actually a finish; Ludwig for a couple years catalogued an outfit of Lavender Pearl drums and referred to it as Rainbow Pearl.	
Red (Pearl)	1994
Red Cortex	1978–1984
Red Frost Classic Coat	1992–1993
Red Sparkle	1936–1984
	1997–
Red Silk	1973–1984
Rosewood	1912–1914
Royal Blue	1998–
Sable (High Gloss Black Lacquer)	1992
Silver, Brushed	1984
Silver Sparkle	1936–1984
	1997–
Silver Silk	1974
Sky Blue Pearl	1962–1984
Stipelgold	1926
Stainless Steel	1978–1980
Star Dust High Gloss Lacquer	1992–
Streaked Opal Pearl	1930–1935
Top Hat	1940–1941
	1999
Turqoise Pearl	1928–1930
Vistalite (see pages 160,161)	1975–1980
	2001–
Yellow Vistalite 1975–1977, Smoky 1978–1980	
Walnut	1912–1929
Walnut Cortex	1973–1984
Walnut Stain (Natural)	1970–1971
White (Pearl)	1994
White Cortex	1974–1984
White Enamel	1923–1950s
White Gloss	1982–
White Lacquer (WFL)	1938–1955
White Marine Pearl	1928–1984
Wine Silk	1984
Yellow Cortex	1978

* Standard and Rocker Series colors listed separately. Dates listed represent catalogue listing dates; actual production dates varied slightly.

LUDWIG

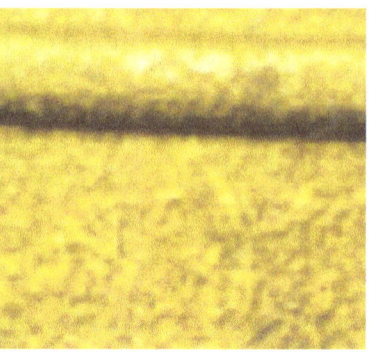

Stipelgold (above) and Ludwigold (below) were both textured finishes. Ludwigold is somewhat similar in appearance to Gold Sparkle, while Stipelgold has a coarser finish and more yellowish hue. Stipelgold snare and bass drums were sold as an outfit with special Stipelgold badges.

Turquoise Pearl

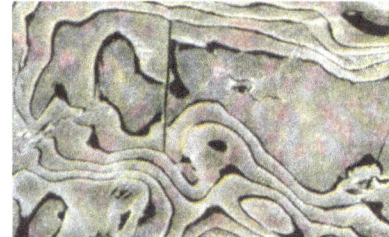

The Abalone Pearl swatch at left (from a Ludwig catalog) closely resembles what the drum below would have looked like before it lost most of its color to fading.

Abalone Pearl

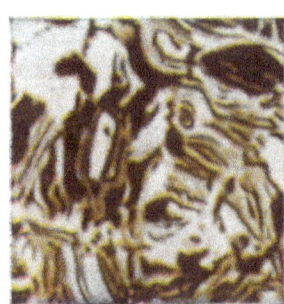

Marble Pearl

Mike Curotto collection

LUDWIG

Lavender Pearl

Emerald Pearl

Streaked Opal Pearl

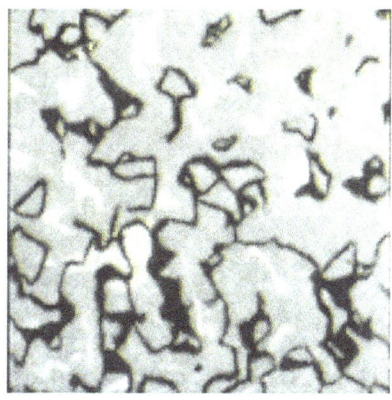

Streaked Opal Pearl, above, was a Ludwig catalogued finish from 1930 to 1935. The drum at left (from the Bun E. Carlos collection) is from October 1935. This finish does not appear in Ludwig catalogs.

PEACOCK PEARL

Ludwig catalogued Peacock Pearl from 1928 to 1932. The author has further broken that down into "Peacock I" (1928–1930) and "Peacock II" (1930–1932).

Peacock II is the same finish that Leedy called Rainbow Pearl. To further complicate matters, Ludwig did not have a finish called Rainbow Pearl, but did catalog an outfit of Lavendar Pearl drums which they named the Rainbow Pearl kit!

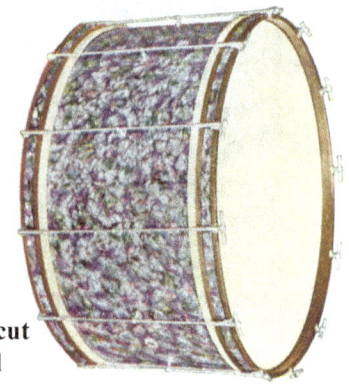

Ludwig catalog cut of Peacock Pearl

Mike Curotto collection

Peacock I

Mike Curotto collection

Peacock II

Peacock II

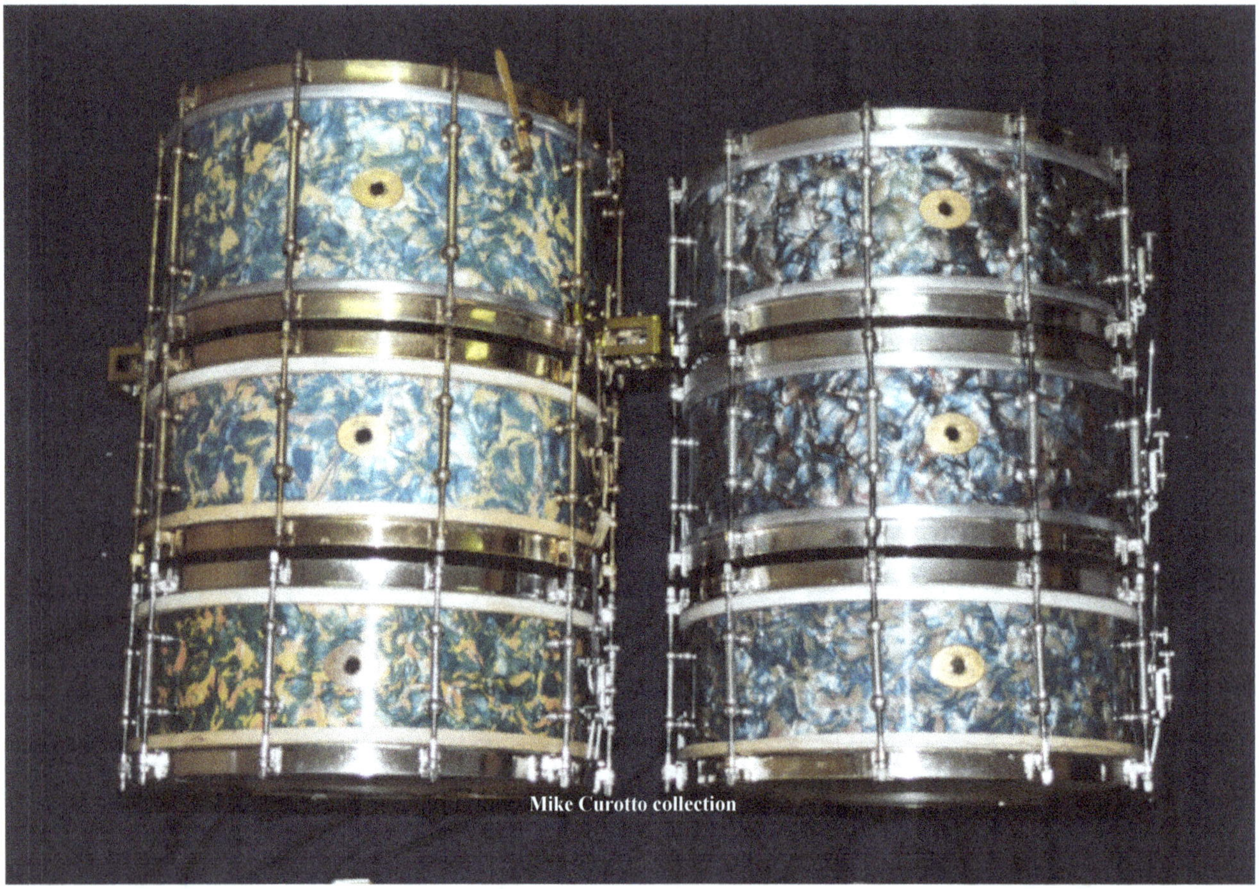

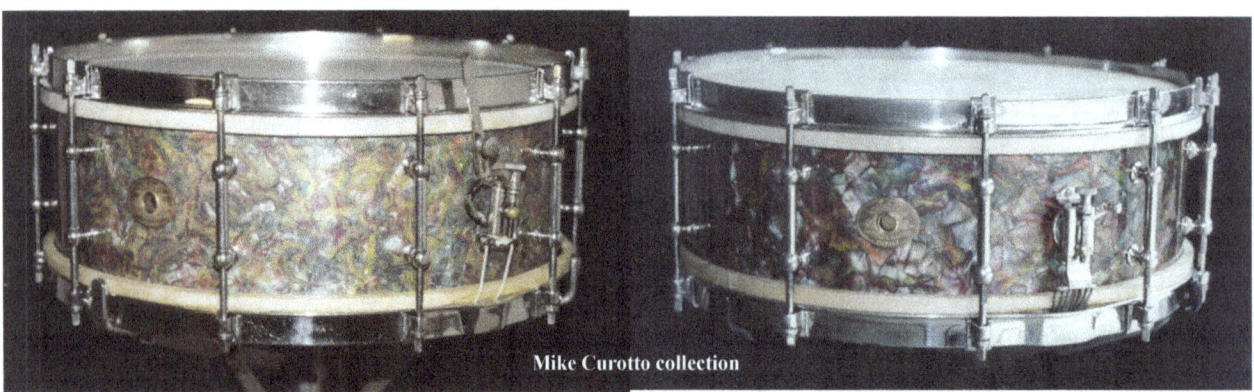

LUDWIG

Among the rarest of the Ludwig finishes is the "Top Hat" found only in the 1940 and 1941 catalogs. The covering of the drum below was electronically scanned in 1998 so the covering pattern could be reproduced (background here) for a limited number of drums.

Photo courtesy Joe Luoma

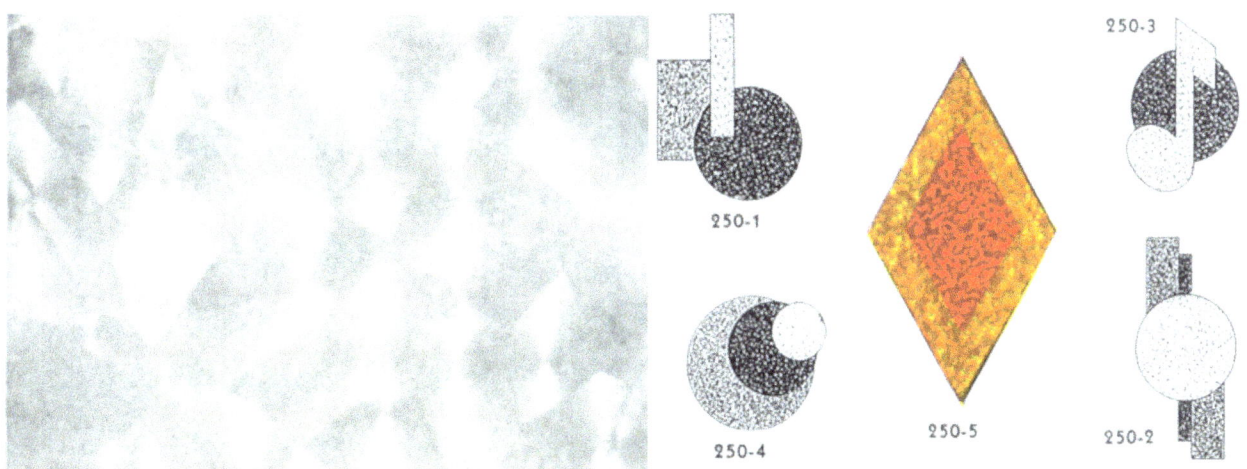

Crystal; another extremely rare finish, shown only in the 1941 catalog.

Flash Pearl Decorations: Optional additions to pearl-covered snare drums, Parade and tenor drums, and bass drums in the late 30s and early 40s.

WFL

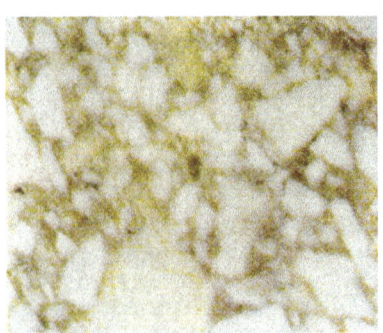
Deluxe Marble
1941

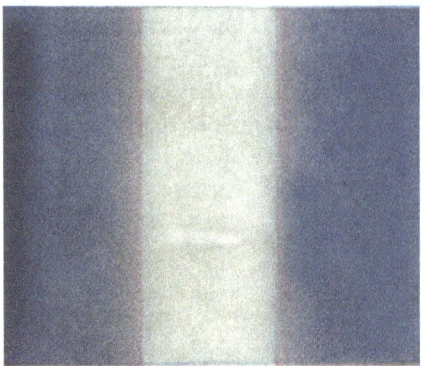
Blue & Silver Lacquer
1939–1955

Black & Gold Lacquer
1939–1955

(Blue and Gold Lacquer was also an option, but not pictured on the color swatch pages of this era.)

WFL experimented with a two-tone pearl covering in the late 1930s and early 1940s. This finish was not listed with the color options although the 1941 catalog did show some drums with this finish.

The finish was rather labor-intensive compared to standard finishes; the pearl covering was special-ordered without a backing; the second color was then sprayed on by hand before applying the covering to the drum.

In addition to black and white marine pearl finishes, WFL had the standard sparkle colors; (from top) Silver, Gold, Green, Red, and Blue.

This tom is from a multi-color WFL kit specially made for a trade show. WFL presented the drums to Johnny Kirkwood who was playing with Louis Jordan at the time. Johnny's son John (also a drummer) now owns the kit.

LUDWIG 1960s ERA FINISHES

The rarest of the 60s colors are the three at the bottom of the page and Galaxy Pearl, at left.

BLACK PANTHER

Oyster Black Pearl

White Marine Pearl

Sparkling Burgundy Pearl

Sparkling Green Pearl

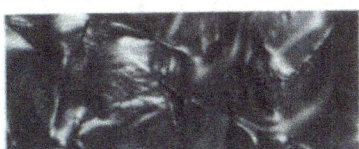
Sparkling Gold Pearl

Black Diamond Pearl

Sparkling Blue Pearl

Sparkling Red Pearl

Oyster Blue Pearl

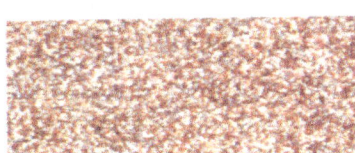
Sparkling Silver Pearl

Sparkling Pink Champagne

Sky Blue Pearl

CITRUS MOD

PSYCHEDELIC RED

MOD ORANGE

LUDWIG

LUDWIG OYSTER FINISHES

Oyster finishes can be among the hardest for collectors to match. The shell at left with no hardware is a '60s Oyster Blue stacked in front of another '60s Oyster blue; the rest of the drums in the photo are Oyster Black. The drum below is what most collectors refer to as the "bowling ball" Oyster Blue. The serial number on this drum is 1906372.

This Oyster Black floor tom does not even match *itself!* The color is uniform, but the design changes so much across the sheet of covering that at the seam it looks like two different drums.

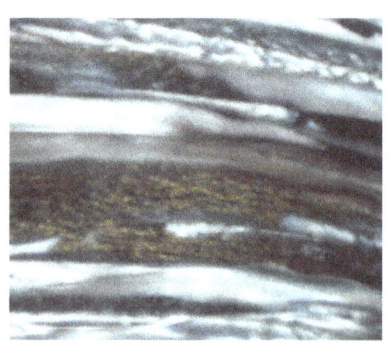

Oyster colors were made up of a swirling of several tints. Occasionally (usually on late '60s drums) there is even an absence of tint leaving patches of mahogany grain peeking through.

"Bowling Ball" Oyster Black
S/N 730768

The rarest of the Oyster finishes; Oyster Pink.
Bun E. Carlos: "Bill Ludwig told me that they made under 100 kits of Oyster Pink between 1958 and 1963; a lot of the kits have been recovered since then. That was not a popular finish."

LUDWIG STANDARD

Silver Astro

Blue Astro

Red Astro   Charcoal Astro   Gold Astro

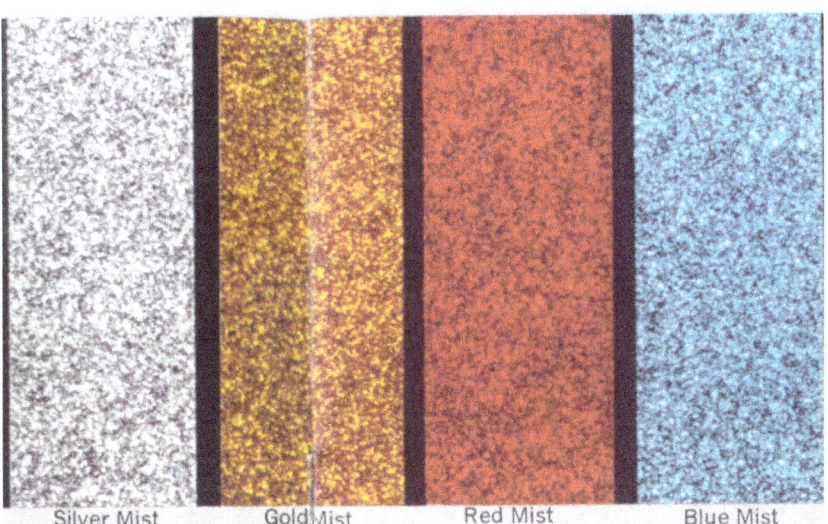
Silver Mist   Gold Mist   Red Mist   Blue Mist

Gold Strata   Blue Strata   Bronze Strata   Ruby Strata   Lemon Strata   Avocado Strata

LUDWIG

LUDWIG 1970s ERA FINISHES

This swatch page is from 1972's catalog #73. In 1974 Gold Silk and Silver Silk were replaced by Black Cortex and White Cortex; solid black and white pyralin coverings.

Bun E. Carlos: "The green in the Psych Red is real unstable. I understand Dow made the pearl for the Keystone (badge) drums and I know a guy who claims that 8 hours in direct sunlight and the green will turn white. The 70s (blue and olive badge) drums are a lot more green now because of this; it's a darker, more stable green to begin with. If you've got 60s Psych Red, don't expose them to sunlight!!"

CHROME FINISH ON WOOD DRUM SHELLS ALSO AVAILABLE

LUDWIG VISTALITE

Vistalite was introduced in 1973 (some sources cite 1972 and certainly work on the line had begun by then, but Ludwig's introductory letter was sent in early 1973) with six colors; clear, yellow, amber, red, blue, and green. Patterns were introduced in 1975, as were Solid White and Solid Black. Green Vistalite as shown on the next page from a 1975 brochure was replaced with Smoky Vistalite by 1978. (According to William F. Ludwig II, only 50 green Vistalite kits were made in the 1970s.) Pattern options were reduced to A (see next page) by 1979 and Solid White was discontinued about the same time. Solid white did not sell very well. It was therefore a major problem when Ludwig mistakenly triple-ordered a supply of solid white plexiglass from their vendor. To use the material up, Ludwig covered white vistalite shells with chrome covering materal. Vistalite was discontinued in about 1983, with a clear Vistalite 5-piece kit reintroduced in 2000.

These pictures are among the best known Ludwig Vistalite photos, from the cover of catalogs 75 and 75-1. (Collector Frankie V. even recreated the shot below, see page 130.) According to Wm. F. Ludwig III, we will probably never know the identity of the person at the outfit; he was not a drummer, just an employee of the ad agency that prepared the catalog.

LUDWIG

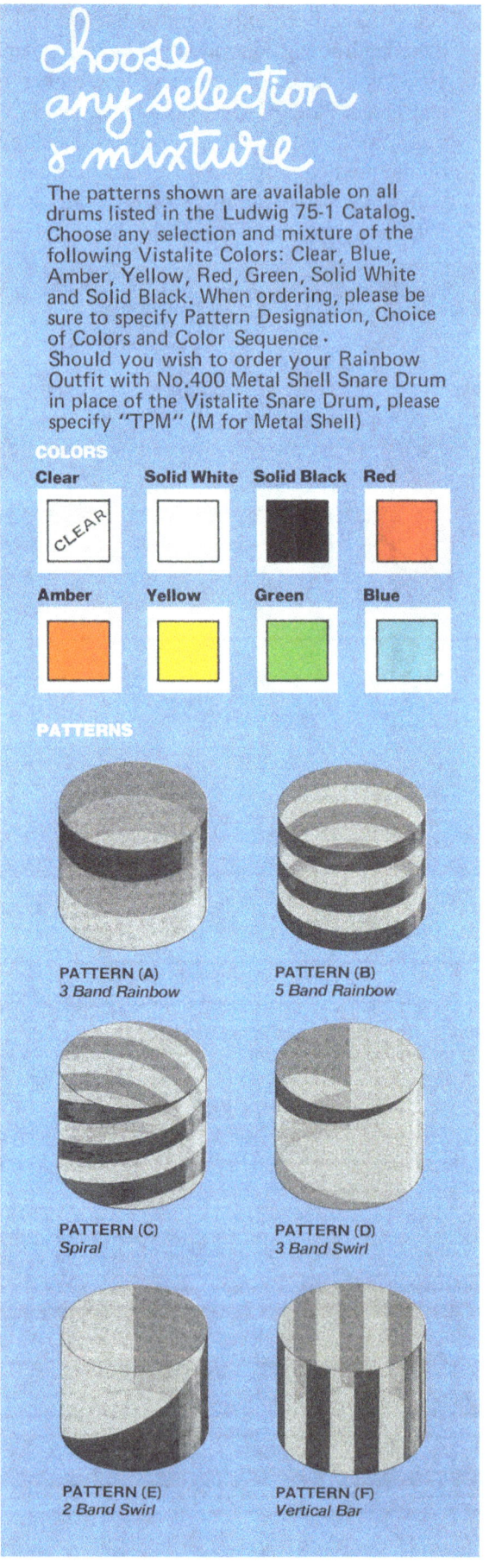

choose any selection & mixture

The patterns shown are available on all drums listed in the Ludwig 75-1 Catalog. Choose any selection and mixture of the following Vistalite Colors: Clear, Blue, Amber, Yellow, Red, Green, Solid White and Solid Black. When ordering, please be sure to specify Pattern Designation, Choice of Colors and Color Sequence.
Should you wish to order your Rainbow Outfit with No. 400 Metal Shell Snare Drum in place of the Vistalite Snare Drum, please specify "TPM" (M for Metal Shell)

COLORS
Clear • Solid White • Solid Black • Red
Amber • Yellow • Green • Blue

PATTERNS
PATTERN (A) 3 Band Rainbow
PATTERN (B) 5 Band Rainbow
PATTERN (C) Spiral
PATTERN (D) 3 Band Swirl
PATTERN (E) 2 Band Swirl
PATTERN (F) Vertical Bar

LUDWIG
1978

THE CLASSIC PEARLS

No. 100 Black Diamond
No. 101 White Marine
No. 102 Oyster Blue
No. 103 Sky Blue
No. 104 Sparkle Silver
No. 105 Sparkle Gold
No. 106 Sparkle Red
No. 107 Sparkle Green
No. 108 Sparkle Blue

THE CORTEX™ CONTEMPORARIES

No. 500 Blue Cortex
No. 501 Red Cortex
No. 502 Yellow Cortex
No. 503 Black Cortex
No. 504 White Cortex
No. 505 Marble Cortex
No. 506 Mahogany Cortex
No. 507 Butcher Block Cortex

THE VISTALITES

No. 300 Blue Vistalite
No. 301 Red Vistalite
No. 302 Amber Vistalite
No. 303 Yellow Vistalite
No. 304 Smoky Vistalite
No. 305 Clear Vistalite
No. 306 Black Vistalite
No. 307 White Vistalite

THE NATURALS

No. 700 Natural Maple Wood
No. 701 Natural Mahogany Wood
No. 720 Chrome-O-Wood
No. 900 Stainless Steel

In the 1978 catalog, customers were encouraged to create their own Multi-sparkle patterns by combining any of up to five sparkle pearl finishes listed, or choose any mixture of 8 Vistalite colors in 4 patterns.

LUDWIG
1984

Natural Finishes — Maple Wood — Mahogany Wood — Natural Walnut

 L-700  L-701 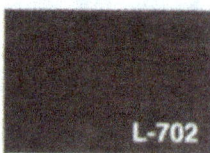 L-702

Color Silks — Silver Silk — Blue Silk — Red Silk — Gold Silk — Wine Silk

 L-114 L-115 L-116  L-117   L-118

Glossy Finishes — Black Gloss — White Gloss — Chrome Pearl — Chrome-O-Wood — Brushed Silver

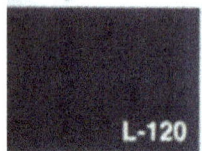 L-120   L-121 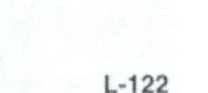 L-122  L-420 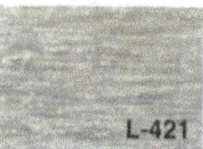 L-421

Cortex Contemporaries — Blue Cortex — Red Cortex — Black Cortex — White Cortex — Mahogany Cortex

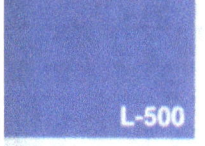 L-500  L-501  L-503 L-504  L-506

Classic Pearls — Black Diamond — White Marine — Sky Blue — Sparkle Silver Brushed Gold

 L-100 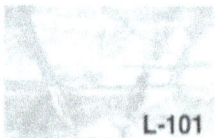 L-101 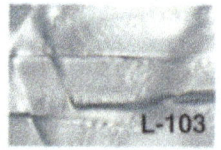 L-103  L-104  L-422

Sparkle Gold — Sparkle Red — Sparkle Green — Sparkle Blue   Butcher Block Cortex

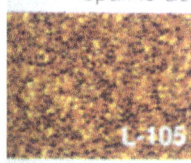 L-105 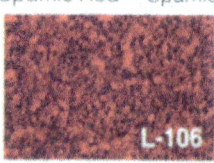 L-106 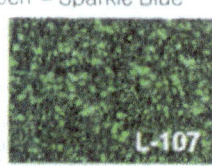 L-107 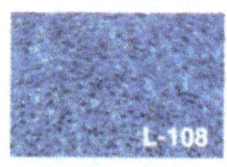 L-108  L-507

75th Anniversary Outfit:
American Eagle Emblems on toms

LUDWIG
LATE 1980s, 1990s

Classic Clear Maple 1988–

Classic Mahogany Stain 1988–1992

Classic Walnut Stain 1988–1992

Mahogany Cortex 1988–1995

White Cortex 1988– 1995

Black Cortex 1988–1995
(renamed Rock Onyx in 1989)

Red Cortex 1988– renamed Plum Crazy in 1989

White Marine Pearl 1988–1989 1995–

1988–1989: named Brushed Silver in 1988, Silver Smoke in 1989

Red Sparkle 1988–1989   1998–

Silver Sparkle 1988–1989   1995–

Blue Sparkle 1988–1989   2000–

Mirrored Chrome 1988–1989

Red Fury 1989

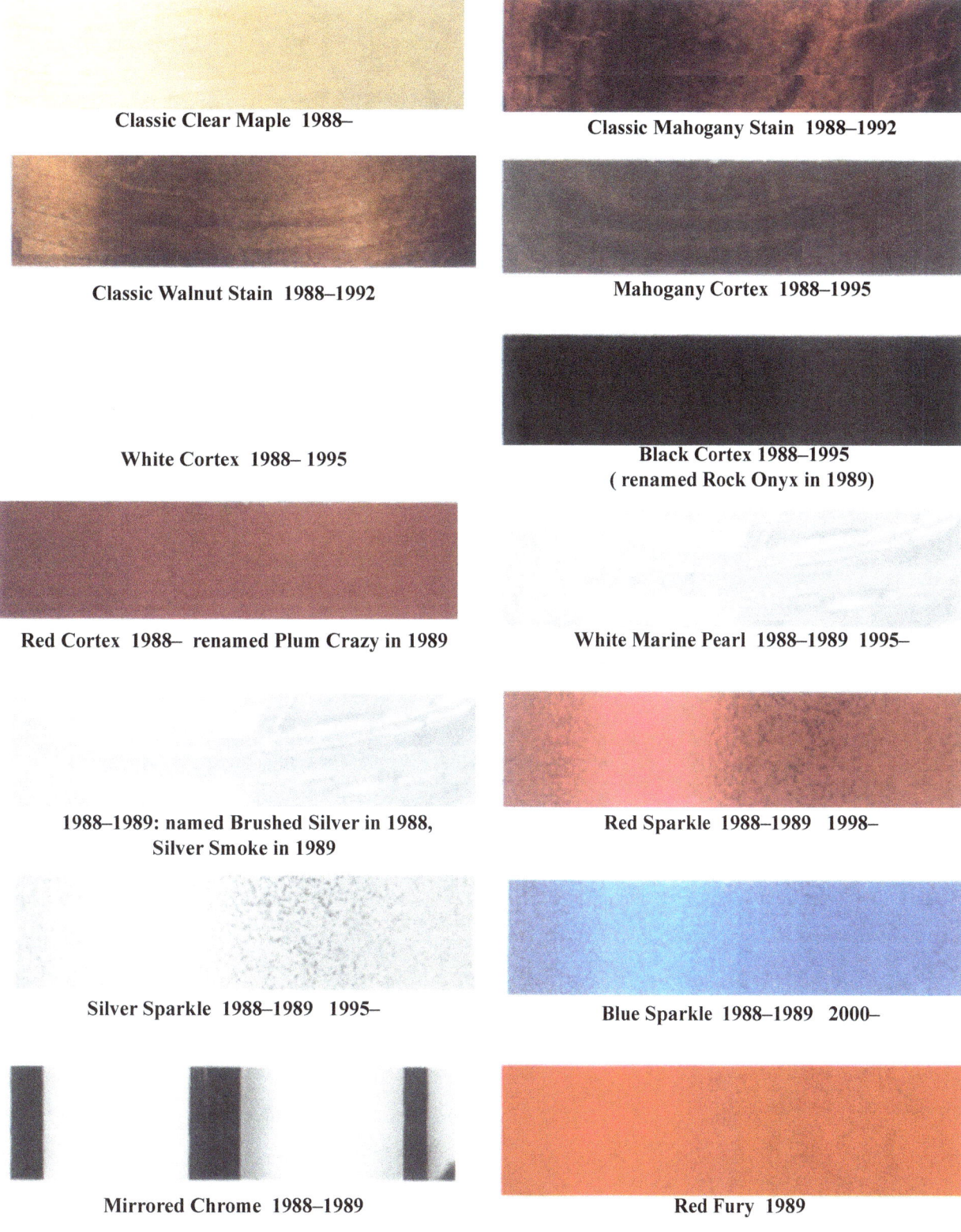

African Satinwood Super Classic series snare drums 1994–

LUDWIG

LUDWIG

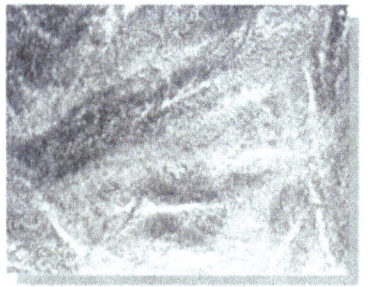
Black

Ivory

Blue

MARBLE FINISHES 1994–1997
Sponge-applied hand-painted lacquer finishes.
UV (ultraviolet light cured) treated, coated with clear polyurethane.

Classic Coat finishes
Baked-on solid color polyurethane. (Interior of shell sealed with clear, high-gloss lacquer.)

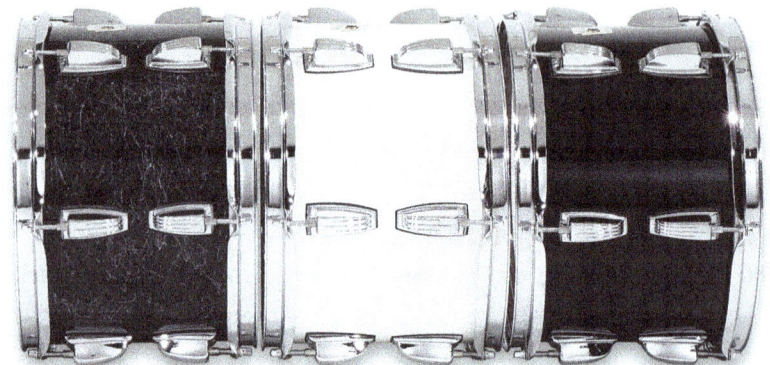

Star Dust 1998– **Arctic 1992–** **Sable 1992–**
(not pictured: Crimson 1992–1993, Red Frost 1992–1993, Blue Frost 1992–1993)

Wrapped Finishes
In 1995 wrapped finishes, which had been offerred only on Rocker Series drums for several years, were brought back on Classic and Super Classic drums.

Black Oyster   **Black Sparkle**   **Purple Sparkle**   **Champagne**   **Black Diamond**
1995–   **1995–**   **1998–**   **1995–**   **1995–**

LUDWIG

Shadow Finishes

Shadow finishes feature a clear, highgloss polyurethane over a hard maple exterior that has been impregnated with dye. Buffed to a mirror finish and hard-baked. The Cherry and Coral finishes below were referred to as "stain" finished rather than "Shadow" finishes. There was no difference from a manufacturing perspective. (Not pictured: Flame, offered in 1992 only.)

Plum 1998–   **Emerald 1993–**   **Black Gold 1998–**   **Purple 1992–**   **Charcoal 1992–**

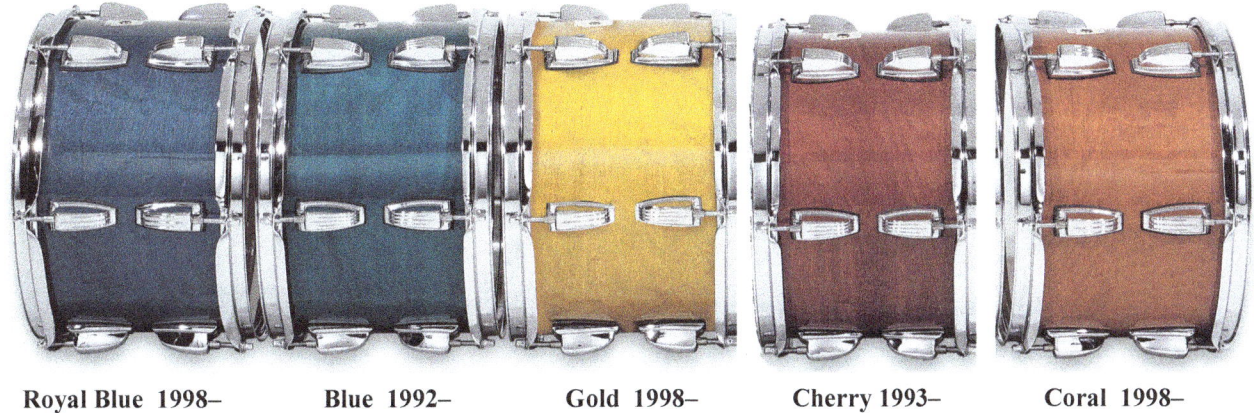

Royal Blue 1998–   **Blue 1992–**   **Gold 1998–**   **Cherry 1993–**   **Coral 1998–**

Re-issue finishes

Psychedelic Red and see-through Vistalite were introduced in 2001, both offered in the Big Beat outfit only.

LUDWIG
ROCKER SERIES FINISHES

Rocker finishes started out with basic solid wraps; the options increased as the line grew in popularity. By the late 1990s there was a complete line of lacquer finishes, solid wraps, and in 2000, a set of sparkle finishes for the Rocker Pro series was introduced. From 1991 through 2000 the finishes offered on Rocker, Rocker II, Rocker Pro, Rocker Elite, and Classic Birch (renamed Rocker Pro) included: Amber, Azure Blue, Black, Black Satin, Black Sparkle, Blue, Black Sparkle, Blue Sparkle, Cherry Wine, Crimson Red, Emerald Green, Gold Sparkle, Hunter Green, Midnight Black, Mirrored Chrome, Natural, Piano Black, Plum Crazy, Red Fury, Red Onyx, Red Sparkle, Rock Onyx (Black), Satin Wine, Sea Blue, Silver Sparkle, Smoke Black, White Frost, & Wine.

1994 Rocker

1998 ROCKER PRO   1998 ROCKER ELITE

LUDWIG

LUDWIG GOLD

The first drum to be gold-plated by Ludwig (c.1916) was this 6.5x14 6-lug drum which was presented to Shelly Manne's father, Max Manne, upon the occasion of his leaving Vernon Castle's orchestra to become production manager of the new Roxy Theatre in New York. This drum is now on display in the Museum of the Percussive Arts Society in Lawton, Oklahoma.

photos courtesy Percussive Arts Society

1923–1928 "All Gold" model (no engraving)

Bun E Carlos collection

photo by Paul Thomas

For about three years (1926–1928) Ludwig catalogued engraved gold-plated snare drums referred to as "Triumphal" models. While there were other models with engraved shells, note that the "Triumphal" also featured engraved hoops and lugs. While thousands of the engraved "Black Beauty" drums were produced by Ludwig in the 1920s and 1930s, the number of gold-plated drums of that era was almost certainly in the hundreds, and the number of gold engraved "Triumphal" models was probably in the dozens. This photo was provided by the drum's owner, Stephen M. Hillman of Massachusetts. Hillman, who is Legal Counsel to Not So Modern Drummer Publications, went to great lengths to verify this drum's authenticity. His research determined that the drum had almost never been used.

LUDWIG

4x14, 8-lug Triumphal from the Mike Curotto collection. Note the unique engraving pattern.

This 5x14, 6-lug drum was produced as a presentation drum; note the smooth oval at the left. This area was clearly never factory-engraved. This drum was acquired by Mike Curotto in 2001. Its listing as an Ebay auction sparked lengthy debates in a prominent vintage drum internet forum. Knowing that Curotto monitored the forum, participants asked for Mike's opinion of the drum, but got no response. The forum's consensus was that the gold finish had been defaced, devaluing the drum. With the bidding in the thousands of dollars, bidders began to get nervous and retract bids. The auction closed with no bids. Mike then contacted the seller and arranged the purchase.

LUDWIG

This 5x14 Triumphal reportedly belonged at one time to a riverboat drummer. It is now in the Mike Curotto collection.

Another unique engraving pattern, on a Triumphal formerly part of William F. Ludwig II's personal collection. This drum was made for silent film star Wm. S. Hart as a gift for his son. It was later replaced by a more elaborate drum with a solid silver shell and solid gold fittings. (The silver drum is still in Hart family possession.) This drum is in the Mike Curotto collection.

LUDWIG

In 1964 Ludwig made four gold-plated super-sensitive presentation drums for Ringo Starr, Bobby Christian, Joe Morello, and Dick Schory who is shown here with his.

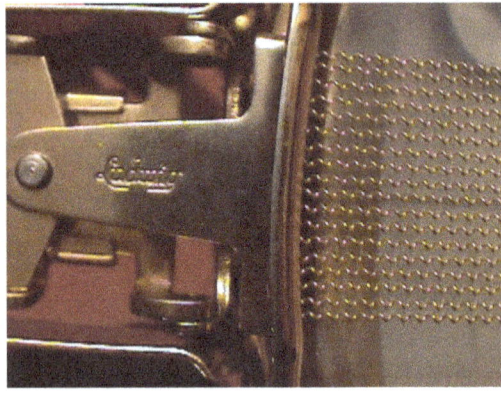

photo courtesy Kevin Dusenbury

Around 1970 Ludwig made 15 Supraphonics triple-plated with 24-K gold as a thank-you to major dealers for huge sales figures. Wm. F. Ludwig II is shown here with Ludwig collector Kevin Dusenbury and one of these drums.

ROGERS

The years listed below represent the years these finishes were listed in Rogers catalogs. These dates should not be construed as the *only* dates these finishes were available; there was often a gap of two to five years between catalog printings.

Scotch Plaid appeared only in a couple of 1950s catalogs and was a finish developed specifically for Bob Reynolds, director of bands at Carnegie Tech. Former marketing director Ben Strauss recalled that the school's band had a Scottish theme (see page 92), with tartans and bagpipes, etc., so at a Rogers salesman's request a plaid finish was made. Strauss remembered this as a contact-paper type of finish as opposed to a pyralin.

Finish	Years
Black Onyx Pearl	1962–1964
Black Oyster (R-360 series)	1968–1972
Black Strata Pearl	1967
Block	1973–1976
Blue Diamond (R-380 series)	1968–1972
Blue Mist	1980–1984
Blue Onyx Pearl	1962–1967
Blue Oyster (R-360 series)	1968–1972
Blue Ripple (R-360 series)	1968–1972
Blue Strata Pearl	1967
California Wine	1980–1984
Combination Pearl	1964–1973
Duco Combination	1958–1964
Duco Ebony	1938
Duco White	1938
Emerald Pearl	1938
KOA	1973–1976
Mahogany	1938
Metallic Gold	1976–1984
Metallic Silver	1976
Mardi Gras Pearl	1958–1962
Midnight Mist	1980–1984
Mojave Red	1973–1976
Natural Maple	1980–1984
New Blonde	1973
New England White	1973–1976
New Mahogany	1972–1976
Pacific Blue	1973–1976
Pearl White	1938–1976
(name changed to white marine pearl in 1958)	
Pearl Black	1938–1973
(name changed to black diamond pearl in 1958)	
Pink Champagne Pearl	1964–1967
Pink Strata Pearl	1967
Platinum	1980–1984
Red Onyx Pearl	1964–1967
Red Oyster (R-380 series)	1968–1972
Red Ripple (R-360 series)	1968–1972
Red Umber (R-360 series)	1968–1972
Scotch Plaid	1958
Sky-blue Ripple Pearl	1960–1962
Solid jet Black Pearl	1958–1976
(name changed to Ebony in 1973)	
Spanish Gold	1976–1984
Sparkling Blue	1958–1967
Sparkling Gold	1938–1967
Sparkling Green	1938–1967
Sparkling Red	1958–1967
Sparkling Silver	1938–1967
Steel-Gray Ripple Pearl	1960–1967
Tobacco Sunburst Lacquer	1979–1984
Wildwood	1967
Wine Red Ripple Pearl	1960–1967

Purple Diamond Pearl: See page 93.

Sunburst: The tobacco sunburst drums were originally produced with dark brown edges, fading to a yellow midsection. When John Cermenaro was working as R&D engineer in the early 1980s, he saw a drum in the paint shop which was unfinished, and faded from the dark brown to a natural midsection. He thought this was an appealing color, and had the paint shop switch. He later realized that this would create problems matching drums to older sets, and had production switch back to yellow in the midsection.

Sparkle note: See page 105 for examples and explanation of Glass vs. non-Glass glitter.

Variations: Patterns such as Ripple, Strata, and Onyx finishes fluctuate quite a bit in both tightness of pattern and contrast. This is primarily due to the pyralin manufacturing process. A few shells were painted black before these translucent coverings were applied, resulting in darker hues.

ROGERS

Wildwood was a which never appeared in a regular Rogers catalog. The color shown here is orange; it was also offered in Green and Blue. This (very thin) veneer was dyed while the tree was still living; fertilizer spikes with tint were driven into the ground, and the tree sucked the color up! See page 44.

SKY-BLUE RIPPLE PEARL	BLACK AND GOLD MULTI-COLOR	BLUE AND SILVER MULTI-COLOR	SPARKLING SILVER PEARL
*COMBINATION	STEEL-GRAY RIPPLE PEARL	WINE-RED RIPPLE PEARL	MARDI GRAS PEARL
RED ONYX PEARL	BLUE ONYX PEARL	BLACK ONYX PEARL	PINK CHAMPAGNE PEARL
BLACK STRATA PEARL	PINK STRATA PEARL	BLUE STRATA PEARL	GREEN SPARKLE PEARL
BLUE SPARKLE PEARL	RED SPARKLE PEARL	GOLD SPARKLE PEARL	BLACK DIAMOND PEARL

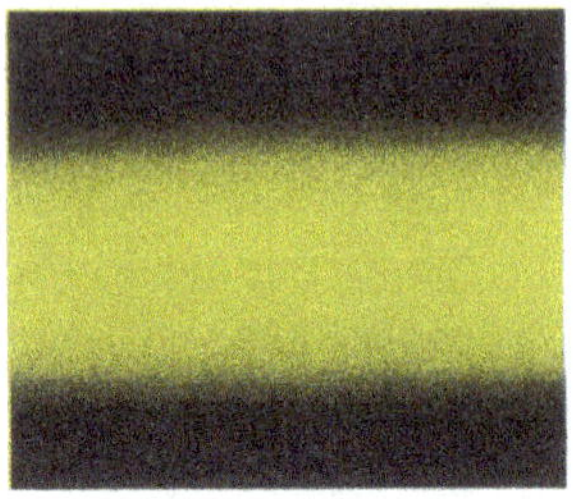

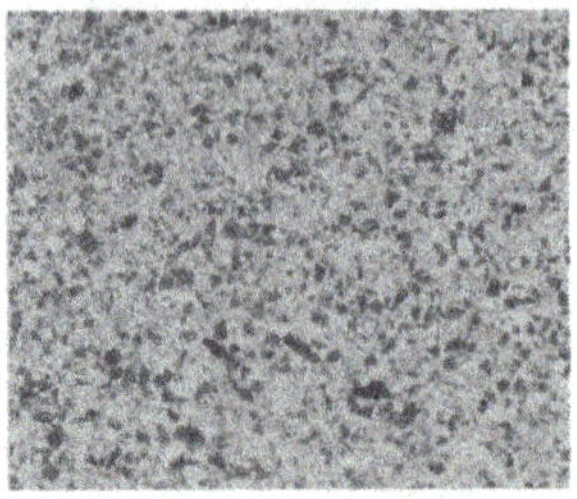

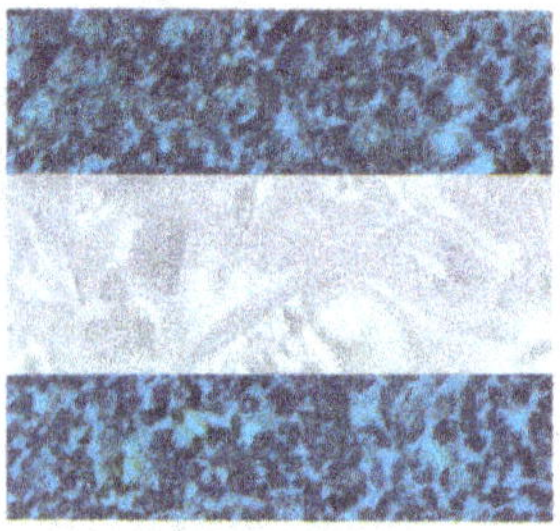

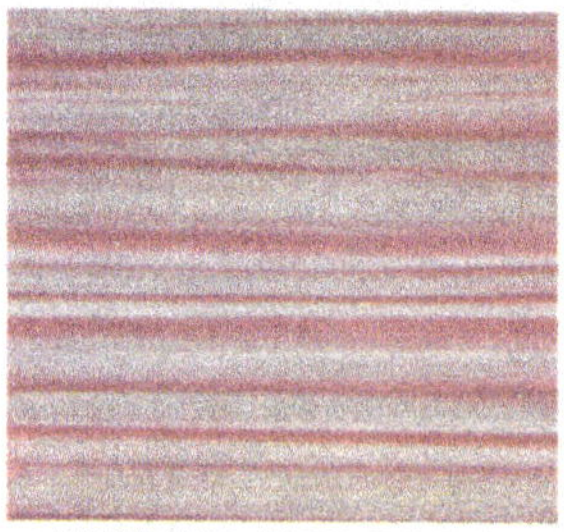

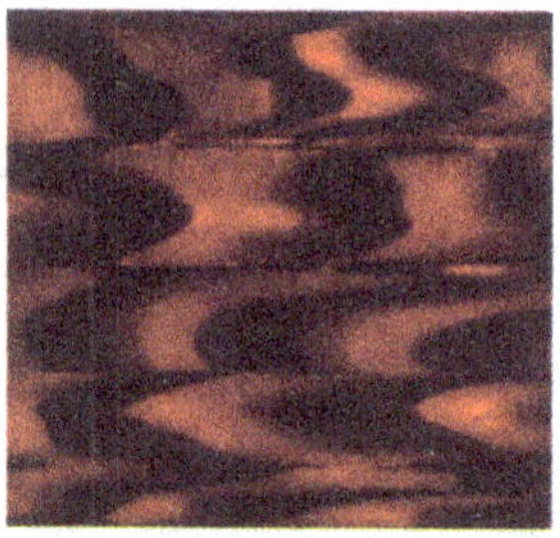

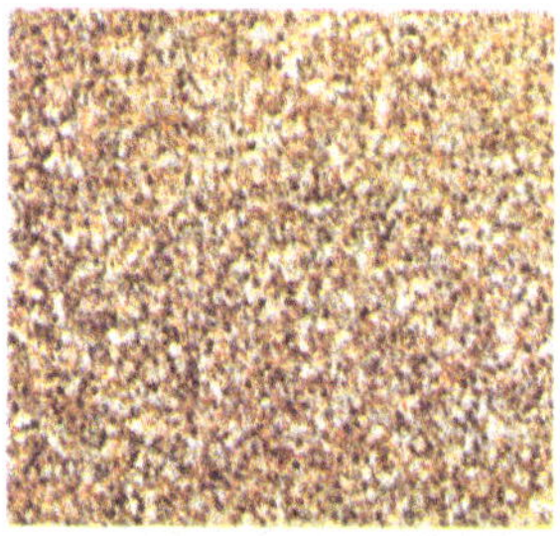

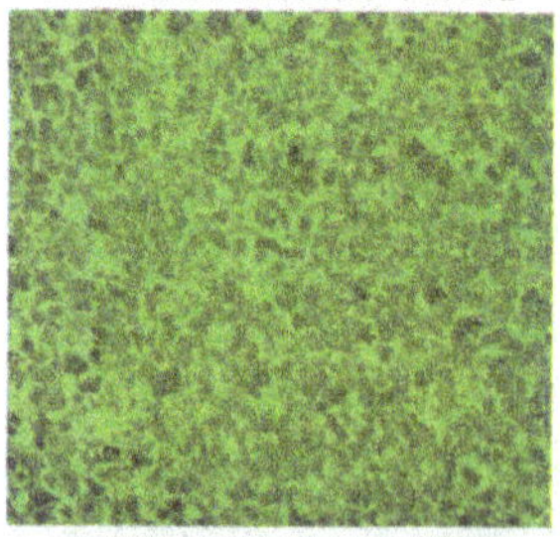

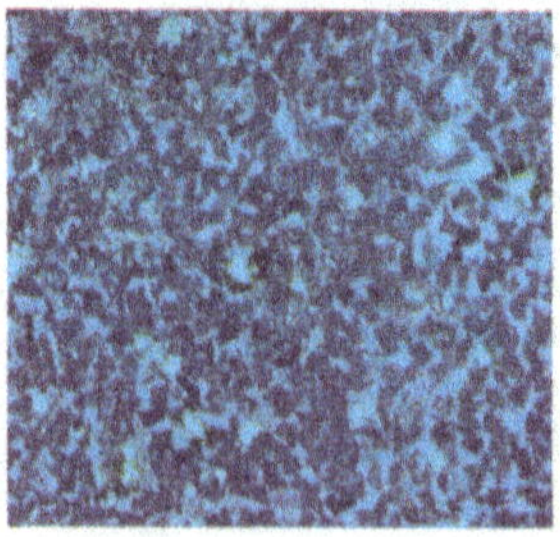

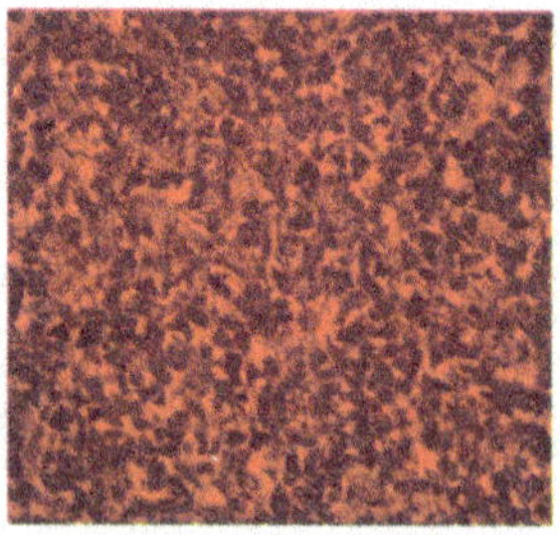

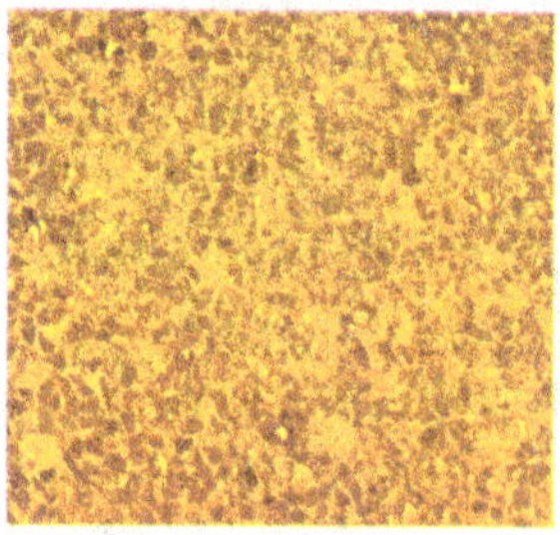

ROGERS

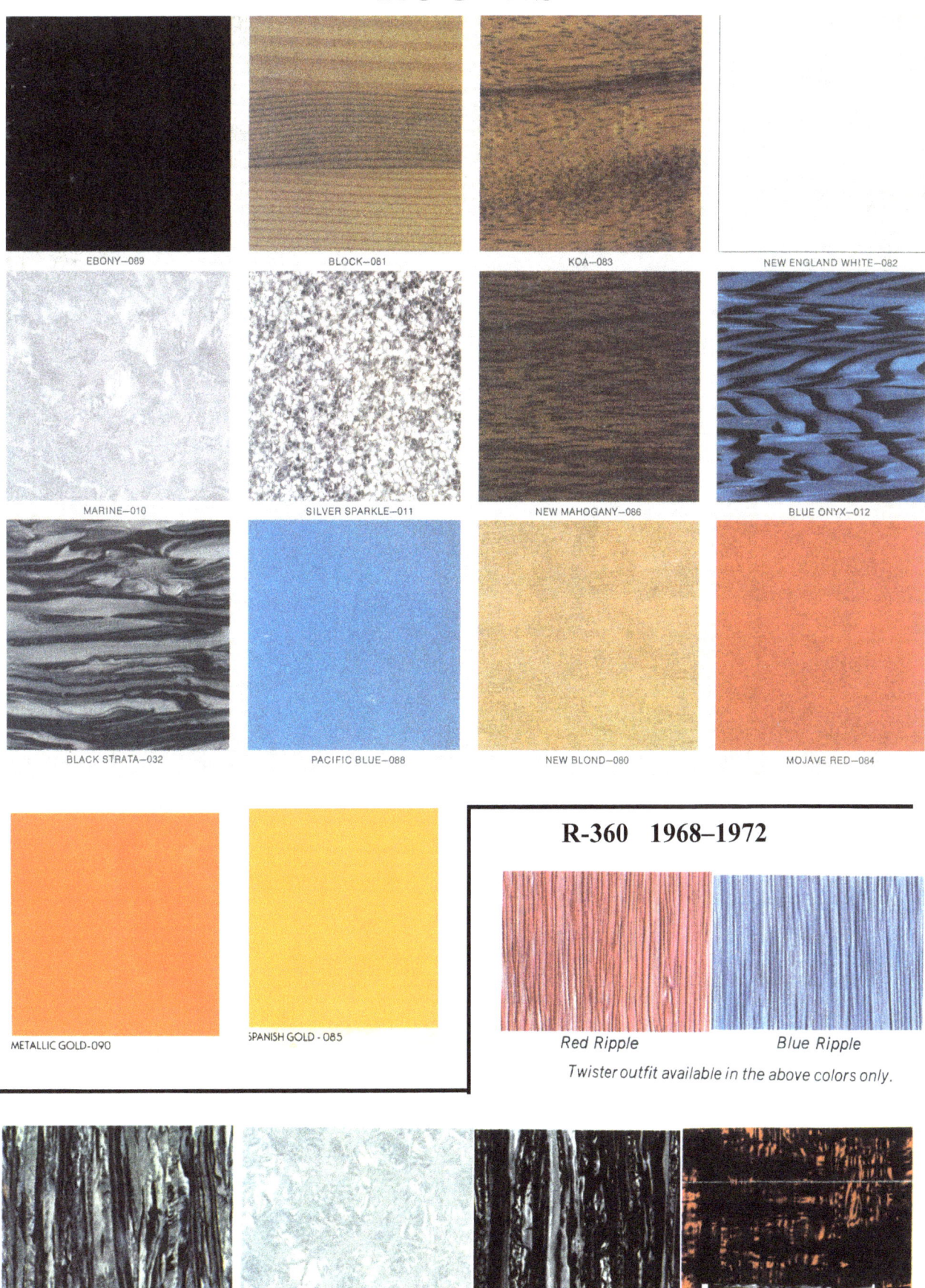

EBONY—089 BLOCK—081 KOA—083 NEW ENGLAND WHITE—082
MARINE—010 SILVER SPARKLE—011 NEW MAHOGANY—086 BLUE ONYX—012
BLACK STRATA—032 PACIFIC BLUE—088 NEW BLOND—080 MOJAVE RED—084
METALLIC GOLD—090 SPANISH GOLD—085

R-360   1968–1972

Red Ripple   Blue Ripple

Twister outfit available in the above colors only.

Double Soul and Rock Solid outfits available in the above colors only.

ROGERS

ROGERS

The Scotch Plaid finish was catalogued only in 1958. The finish was developed specifically for the Carnegie Tech Kiltie Band (below,) but added to the catalog. Sales were slow, and the finish was soon discontinued.

drum photos courtesy Gary Nelson

ROGERS

photo courtesy NotSoModernDrummer magazine

Purple Diamond Pearl

This color was never catalogued and when the author questioned him before his death Ben Strauss did not remember this finish. Still, there evidently were a fair number of drums produced in this finish over the space of at least several years. Collector Gary Nelson of New Jersey has accumulated a number of drums with this finish, with distinctively different vintages of hardware features, badges, etc.

Nelson heard about the finish before he ever saw one, and began searching for one to determine whether it was simply a faded Black Diamond Pearl. Removing a lug proved that the original color was a vibrant purple.

All drums on this page are from the collection of Gary Nelson.

photo by Gary Nelson

photo by Gary Nelson

ROGERS

  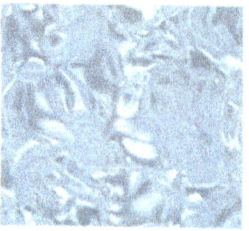 

RED OYSTER JET BLACK MARINE PEARL BLUE DIAMOND

R-380 Series, 1968–1972

R-360 Series c.1980

1980s, left to right, top to bottom:
Mojave Red, Midnight Mist
Tobacco Sunburst, Metallic Silver, California Wine
Blue Mist, Ebony, Natural Maple, Metallic Gold
New England White, Platinum, KOA

SLINGERLAND

Black Diamond Pearl
1928–1995

Marine Pearl
1928–1994

Sparkling Red
1934–1986

Opal Pearl
1929–1938
Also referred to as Peacock Pearl (1936).

Mahogany
1928–1986

Walnut
1928–1939 1976–1986

Brilliant Gold
Called sparkling gold after 1929.
1928–1979

Sea Green
1928–1938

Lavender
1929

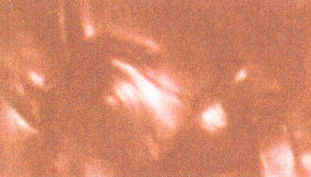
Rose Pearl
1929

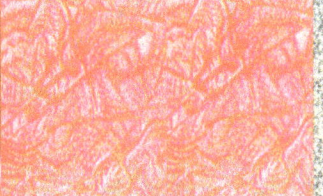
Coral Pearl
1934–1938

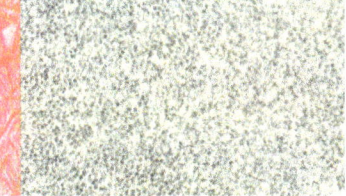
Sparkling Silver
1934–1986

The finish at left can probably best be described as a "Brown Abalone." This was not a catalogued finish and to date the author is unaware of any other example of the finish. This drum belongs to (and photo supplied by) Mike Curotto.

Abalone Pearl
1936

Antique
1934–1938

Two colors of lacquer are actually used for each Antique finish. In 1936 the following color combinations were available at no additional charge from the regular prices: Silver & Blue or Gold & Blue, Silver & Black or Gold & Black. Other colors (sometimes more than two per drum) were certainly applied, and this technique continued through the late 1960s, though the term "Antique finish" appears in Slingerland catalogs only until 1938.

SLINGERLAND

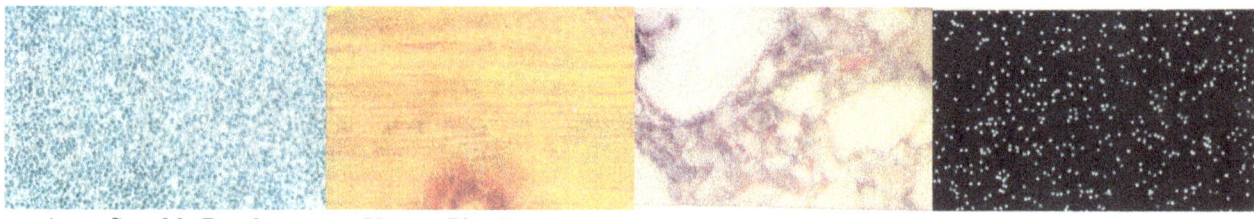

Aqua Sparkle Pearl
1959

Knotty Pine Lacquer
1955–1957

Marble Lacquer
1955 - 1957

Black Sparkle
1958–1967

Outfits were catalogued until 1962 (Knotty Pine) and 1963 (Marble), but neither was listed in color swatch charts after 1957. Knotty Pine was reportedly developed specifically for Krupa, to match his basement paneling.

Capri Pearl
1958–1963

Gold Veiled Ebony Pearl
1958–1963

Silver Veil Pearl
1958–1960

Turquoise Veil Pearl
1958–1960

  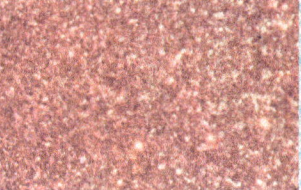 

Smokey (Sparkling) Pearl
1958–1960

Light Blue Pearl
1958–1979

Sparkling Pink
1959–1967

Blue Ripple
1961–1967

 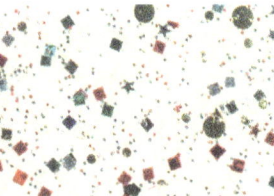  

Oyster Pink
1961–1967

Fiesta
1961–1967

Sparkling Pink Champagne
1961–1973

Combination Pearl finishes
1961–1973
(any two of the seven sparkles)

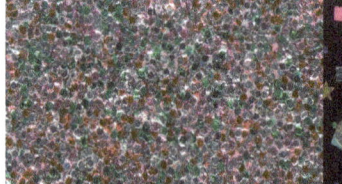 

Sparkling Peacock
1961–1963

Mardi Gras Pearl
1961–1963

Root Beer? Brown Sparkle?
An uncatalogued 1960s finish
Photo courtesy of Lowell Schiff

Blue Satin Flame
1964–1977

Gold Satin Flame
1964–1977

58   Slingerland

SLINGERLAND

Green Satin Flame 1964–1973	Red Satin Flame 1964–1977	Red Ripple 1965–1967	White Satin Flame 1967
Blue Agate Pearl 1965–1977	Black Sparkle 1960–1968	Grey Agate Pearl 1956–1967	Yellow Tiger 1968
Copper 1973	Lavendar Satin Flame Pearl 1970–1973	Red Gloss 1976–1986	Red Tiger Pearl 1970–1973
White Tiger Pearl 1973 - 1977	Sparkling Maroon Pearl 1973	Sparkling OrangePearl 1970–1973	Sparkling Purple Pearl 1970–1973

   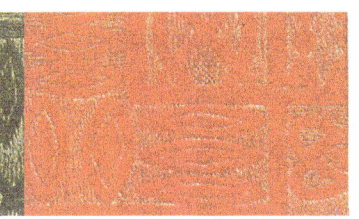

| Tangerine Satin Flame Pearl 1973 | Brown Aztec 1976 | Green Aztec 1976 | Red Aztec 1976 |

| Yellow Aztec 1976 | White Aztec 1976 | Sparkling Green 1934–1986 |

SLINGERLAND

SLINGERLAND-LEEDY COLORS

From 1955 through 1958, the color options for Slingerland's Leedy drums were the same as they'd been in the last Leedy & Ludwig catalog; White Pearl, Black Pearl, Red Sparkle, Blue Sparkle, Gold Sparkle, Silver Sparkle, and Green Sparkle.

In catalog #62 the following colors were added: Black Beauty (solid black pearl), Capri Pearl, Fiesta, Light Blue Pearl, Mardi Gras Pearl, Sparkling Peacock Pearl, Sparkling Pink.

The color swatch page for the Leedy #70 catalog was exactly the same as Slingerland catalog #67.

SLINGERLAND

In the 1970s, the drum finishes Slingerland offered were literally limitless. The acrylic and denim on this page as well as the cordova finishes on the next page were standard finishes. Slingerland even offered to cover drums with artwork of the drummer's choice. To demonstrate and dramatize the possibilities, they showed an outfit at the annual NAMm show which was covered with the Coca-Cola trade-mark.

SLINGERLAND

GREGG POTTER

Slingerland

"This was from when I was doing a lot of stuff with Steve Dahl. He always wore really loud Hawaiian shirts, and Spencer [Aloisio] told me "We can make you a drum that'll be as loud as his shirts!" They only had enough of this material to do this snare for me and a floor tom. I wanted a whole outfit, but it couldn't be done."

Gregg Potter

SLINGERLAND

This unique Slingerland outfit was made in 1979. According to Larry Linkin, who was president at the time, the idea originated with West Coast sales representative Phil Hulsey. Helsey told Link about a guy out in California who was doing remarkable inlay work on custom surfboards. The next time Link was in California they went to the surf shop and Link was equally impressed with the craftsmanship of the wood inlay work. He commissioned enough inlaid veneer to cover a complete set of drums. The drums turned out beautifully, but the cost of producing this prototype outfit was too high to consider making this a regular production item. The outfit remained on the shelf until Link was leaving Slingerland. Shortly before his departure, he called Brian Callahan to his office. Callahan had worked in quality control and product development, working on projects such as the TDR, the marching vibes, and cutaways. Link explained that he was leaving and wanted to give a few key people an opportunity to speak up if there was anything in the way of equipment that he could help them with before he left. Callahan immediately asked about the custom inlaid outfit which he had been impressed with when it was being made. Link let Callahan purchase the outfit for the cost of materials and labor.

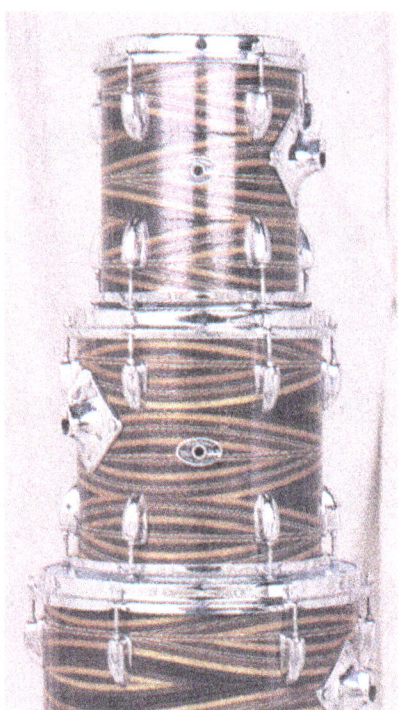

BRIAN CALLAHAN

BLACK GOLD

Black Gold was a gold-tone brass plating for stands and hardware developed in the early '80s. Black Gold was not around long enough to make it into a regular Slingerland catalog; this art is from the flier sent to dealers.

A huge product roll-out was presented at a NAMM show, complete with beautiful models in sexy black and gold tuxedo outfits. The hoopla only served to call attention to the rather spectacular flop.

SLINGERLAND 63

SLINGERLAND
HSS ERA FINISHES

SA-3008C-WR (Wine Red) with SH3000

SA-3062C-BB (Bright Blue) with SH3000 hardware pack.

SA-3000C-NM (Natural Maple) with SH1000 hardware pack.

Artist Series: Shown– Wine Red Maple, Bright Blue, Emerald Green, Natural Maple. Also; Graphite Metallic, White Gloss, Black Gloss. Also, in 1993–1994, Black Diamond Pearl, White Marine Pearl

Spirit Series

| MTS METALLIC SILVER (Spirit only) | W WHITE (Spirit only) | MTB METALLIC BLUE (Spirit only) | MTR METALLIC RED (Spirit & Spirit Plus) | B BLACK (Spirit & Spirit Plus) | CH CHROME (Spirit Plus only) | DKB DARK BLUE (Spirit Plus only) |

SLINGERLAND
GIBSON 1990s FINISHES

For the somewhat limited time period that Gibson distributed the Spirit and Artist Custom drums, they supplied them in the same colors as HSS plus added Dark Walnut and Antique Maple to the Artist Custom. Finishes included coverings, classic urethanes, basic classic colors, and grain-enhanced options. Many of the grain-enhanced finishes and sunburst finishes were the direct result of the efforts of ace drum finisher Pat Foley.

Sunbursts
Amber Burst, Cherry Burst, Tobacco Burst, Green Maple Frost

Stains
Antique Duco White, Emerald Green, Caribbean Nights, Natural Maple, Cherry Mahogany, Wild Cherry, Raven Blue, Grain-enhanced Purple

Classic Wraps
White Satin Flame, Aqua Satin Flame, Gold Satin Flame, Purple Satin Flame, Gold Sparkle, Marine Pearl, Blue Sparkle, Red Sparkle, Green Sparkle, Black Diamond

Solid Colors
Custom Yellow, Jet Black, Gulf Coast Green, Big Band Blue, Coastal Coral, Antique Ivory

Classic - Preferred by history's greatest drummers, including Gene Krupa and Buddy Rich. Pearls or sparkles are available (see price list for details).

Professional hand-rubbed satin - This natural, earthy finish puts less between you and your drum shell. Get the look of a premium finish, at less cost. A popular choice!

Premium - Layers and layers of lacquer are applied and buffed to a deep lustre. Only Slingerland gives you a guitar-quality finish on drums! Available in painted and stained versions.

Signature - Pat Foley's distinctive bursts and fades take drum finishes to a new level. These are the world's most beautiful drum finishes, bar none.

Custom - Pat Foley will design and produce the drums of your dreams (or imagination). Each job is one-of-a-kind, by the master.

Select - Your choice of finish on specially selected highly figured shells.

Pat Foley's Studio King Finishes. The drum shown with the Custom finish was part of the outfit Foley made for Gibson to benefit victims of Montseraat's volcanic disaster. The kit, signed by George Martin, was auctioned off at London's Hard Rock Cafe.

SLINGERLAND
2003 Conway, Arkansas

Tour King Series   Classic V, Black Marine Pearl wrap

Tour King Series   Classic V, Champagne Sparkle wrap

Tour King Series   New Standard, Black Marine Pearl wrap

Tour King Series   Modern Jazz, Green Glitter wrap

Tour King Series Modern Jazz, Red Glitter wrap

**Studio King Series   Rolling Thunder,
Translucent Violet High Gloss Lacquer**

photos courtesy Gibson

REBEATS PUBLICATIONS
visit the Rebeats website or contact us for details

THE GRETSCH DRUM BOOK
by Rob Cook
with John Sheridan
Business history,
dating guide

THE SLINGERLAND BOOK
by Rob Cook
Business history,
dating guide

THE ROGERS BOOK
by Rob Cook
Business history,
dating guide

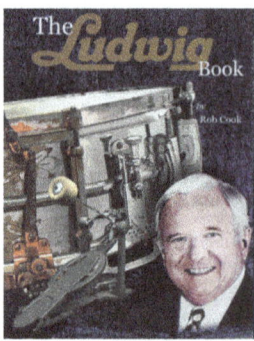
THE LUDWIG BOOK
by Rob Cook
Business history,
dating guide

THE MAKING OF A DRUM COMPANY
The autobiography Wm. F. Ludwig II, with Rob Cook

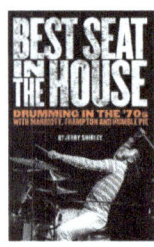
BEST SEAT IN THE HOUSE
Memoir of Humble Pie's Jerry Shirley

THE LEEDY WAY
Biography of George Way, History of Leedy, Camco, Conn, L&S

MY LIFE IN PERCUSSION
Five Decades In The Music Products Industry
Karl Dustman memoir

HAL BLAINE & THE WRECKING CREW
Memoir of Hal Blaine, with Mr. Bonzai

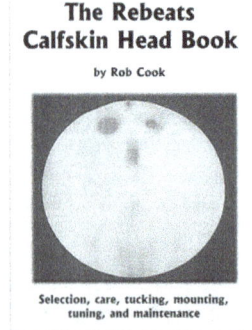
THE REBEATS CALFSKIN HEAD BOOK

George Way mini-biography, vendor directory

GENE KRUPA, HIS LIFE AND TIMES
biography of Gene Krupa, by Bruce Crowther

THE BABY DODDS STORY
Memoir of Baby Dodds, as told to Larry Gara

Gretsch 1941 Catalog Reprint

P.O. Box 6, Alma, Michigan 48801
989 463 4757
www.Rebeats.com   rob@rebeats.com